Vatican II: A Very Short Introduction

VERY SHORT INTRODUCTIONS are for anyone wanting a stimulating and accessible way into a new subject. They are written by experts, and have been translated into more than 45 different languages.

The series began in 1995, and now covers a wide variety of topics in every discipline. The VSI library currently contains over 700 volumes—a Very Short Introduction to everything from Psychology and Philosophy of Science to American History and Relativity—and continues to grow in every subject area.

Very Short Introductions available now:

ABOLITIONISM Richard S. Newman
THE ABRAHAMIC RELIGIONS Charles L. Cohen
ACCOUNTING Christopher Nobes
ADDICTION Keith Humphreys
ADOLESCENCE Peter K. Smith
THEODOR W. ADORNO Andrew Bowie
ADVERTISING Winston Fletcher
AERIAL WARFARE Frank Ledwidge
AESTHETICS Bence Nanay
AFRICAN AMERICAN RELIGION Eddie S. Glaude Jr
AFRICAN HISTORY John Parker and Richard Rathbone
AFRICAN POLITICS Ian Taylor
AFRICAN RELIGIONS Jacob K. Olupona
AGEING Nancy A. Pachana
AGNOSTICISM Robin Le Poidevin
AGRICULTURE Paul Brassley and Richard Soffe
ALEXANDER THE GREAT Hugh Bowden
ALGEBRA Peter M. Higgins
AMERICAN BUSINESS HISTORY Walter A. Friedman
AMERICAN CULTURAL HISTORY Eric Avila
AMERICAN FOREIGN RELATIONS Andrew Preston
AMERICAN HISTORY Paul S. Boyer
AMERICAN IMMIGRATION David A. Gerber
AMERICAN INTELLECTUAL HISTORY Jennifer Ratner-Rosenhagen
THE AMERICAN JUDICIAL SYSTEM Charles L. Zelden
AMERICAN LEGAL HISTORY G. Edward White
AMERICAN MILITARY HISTORY Joseph T. Glatthaar
AMERICAN NAVAL HISTORY Craig L. Symonds
AMERICAN POETRY David Caplan
AMERICAN POLITICAL HISTORY Donald Critchlow
AMERICAN POLITICAL PARTIES AND ELECTIONS L. Sandy Maisel
AMERICAN POLITICS Richard M. Valelly
THE AMERICAN PRESIDENCY Charles O. Jones
THE AMERICAN REVOLUTION Robert J. Allison
AMERICAN SLAVERY Heather Andrea Williams
THE AMERICAN SOUTH Charles Reagan Wilson
THE AMERICAN WEST Stephen Aron
AMERICAN WOMEN'S HISTORY Susan Ware
AMPHIBIANS T. S. Kemp
ANAESTHESIA Aidan O'Donnell
ANALYTIC PHILOSOPHY Michael Beaney
ANARCHISM Alex Prichard

ANCIENT ASSYRIA Karen Radner
ANCIENT EGYPT Ian Shaw
ANCIENT EGYPTIAN ART AND ARCHITECTURE Christina Riggs
ANCIENT GREECE Paul Cartledge
THE ANCIENT NEAR EAST Amanda H. Podany
ANCIENT PHILOSOPHY Julia Annas
ANCIENT WARFARE Harry Sidebottom
ANGELS David Albert Jones
ANGLICANISM Mark Chapman
THE ANGLO-SAXON AGE John Blair
ANIMAL BEHAVIOUR Tristram D. Wyatt
THE ANIMAL KINGDOM Peter Holland
ANIMAL RIGHTS David DeGrazia
ANSELM Thomas Williams
THE ANTARCTIC Klaus Dodds
ANTHROPOCENE Erle C. Ellis
ANTISEMITISM Steven Beller
ANXIETY Daniel Freeman and Jason Freeman
THE APOCRYPHAL GOSPELS Paul Foster
APPLIED MATHEMATICS Alain Goriely
THOMAS AQUINAS Fergus Kerr
ARBITRATION Thomas Schultz and Thomas Grant
ARCHAEOLOGY Paul Bahn
ARCHITECTURE Andrew Ballantyne
THE ARCTIC Klaus Dodds and Jamie Woodward
HANNAH ARENDT Dana Villa
ARISTOCRACY William Doyle
ARISTOTLE Jonathan Barnes
ART HISTORY Dana Arnold
ART THEORY Cynthia Freeland
ARTIFICIAL INTELLIGENCE Margaret A. Boden
ASIAN AMERICAN HISTORY Madeline Y. Hsu
ASTROBIOLOGY David C. Catling
ASTROPHYSICS James Binney
ATHEISM Julian Baggini
THE ATMOSPHERE Paul I. Palmer
AUGUSTINE Henry Chadwick
JANE AUSTEN Tom Keymer
AUSTRALIA Kenneth Morgan
AUTISM Uta Frith
AUTOBIOGRAPHY Laura Marcus
THE AVANT GARDE David Cottington
THE AZTECS Davíd Carrasco
BABYLONIA Trevor Bryce
BACTERIA Sebastian G. B. Amyes
BANKING John Goddard and John O. S. Wilson
BARTHES Jonathan Culler
THE BEATS David Sterritt
BEAUTY Roger Scruton
LUDWIG VAN BEETHOVEN Mark Evan Bonds
BEHAVIOURAL ECONOMICS Michelle Baddeley
BESTSELLERS John Sutherland
THE BIBLE John Riches
BIBLICAL ARCHAEOLOGY Eric H. Cline
BIG DATA Dawn E. Holmes
BIOCHEMISTRY Mark Lorch
BIOGEOGRAPHY Mark V. Lomolino
BIOGRAPHY Hermione Lee
BIOMETRICS Michael Fairhurst
ELIZABETH BISHOP Jonathan F. S. Post
BLACK HOLES Katherine Blundell
BLASPHEMY Yvonne Sherwood
BLOOD Chris Cooper
THE BLUES Elijah Wald
THE BODY Chris Shilling
NIELS BOHR J. L. Heilbron
THE BOOK OF COMMON PRAYER Brian Cummings
THE BOOK OF MORMON Terryl Givens
BORDERS Alexander C. Diener and Joshua Hagen
THE BRAIN Michael O'Shea
BRANDING Robert Jones
THE BRICS Andrew F. Cooper
BRITISH CINEMA Charles Barr
THE BRITISH CONSTITUTION Martin Loughlin
THE BRITISH EMPIRE Ashley Jackson
BRITISH POLITICS Tony Wright
BUDDHA Michael Carrithers
BUDDHISM Damien Keown
BUDDHIST ETHICS Damien Keown

BYZANTIUM Peter Sarris
CALVINISM Jon Balserak
ALBERT CAMUS Oliver Gloag
CANADA Donald Wright
CANCER Nicholas James
CAPITALISM James Fulcher
CATHOLICISM Gerald O'Collins
CAUSATION Stephen Mumford and Rani Lill Anjum
THE CELL Terence Allen and Graham Cowling
THE CELTS BarryCunliffe
CHAOS Leonard Smith
GEOFFREY CHAUCER David Wallace
CHEMISTRY Peter Atkins
CHILD PSYCHOLOGY Usha Goswami
CHILDREN'S LITERATURE Kimberley Reynolds
CHINESE LITERATURE Sabina Knight
CHOICE THEORY Michael Allingham
CHRISTIAN ART Beth Williamson
CHRISTIAN ETHICS D. Stephen Long
CHRISTIANITY Linda Woodhead
CIRCADIAN RHYTHMS Russell Foster and Leon Kreitzman
CITIZENSHIP Richard Bellamy
CITY PLANNING Carl Abbott
CIVIL ENGINEERING David Muir Wood
CLASSICAL LITERATURE William Allan
CLASSICAL MYTHOLOGY Helen Morales
CLASSICS Mary Beard and John Henderson
CLAUSEWITZ Michael Howard
CLIMATE Mark Maslin
CLIMATE CHANGE Mark Maslin
CLINICAL PSYCHOLOGY Susan Llewelyn and Katie Aafjes-van Doorn
COGNITIVE BEHAVIOURAL THERAPY Freda McManus
COGNITIVE NEUROSCIENCE Richard Passingham
THE COLD WAR Robert J. McMahon
COLONIAL AMERICA Alan Taylor
COLONIAL LATIN AMERICAN LITERATURE Rolena Adorno
COMBINATORICS Robin Wilson
COMEDY Matthew Bevis
COMMUNISM Leslie Holmes
COMPARATIVE LITERATURE Ben Hutchinson
COMPETITION AND ANTITRUST LAW Ariel Ezrachi
COMPLEXITY John H. Holland
THE COMPUTER Darrel Ince
COMPUTER SCIENCE Subrata Dasgupta
CONCENTRATION CAMPS Dan Stone
CONDENSED MATTER PHYSICS Ross H. McKenzie
CONFUCIANISM Daniel K. Gardner
THE CONQUISTADORS Matthew Restall and Felipe Fernández-Armesto
CONSCIENCE Paul Strohm
CONSCIOUSNESS Susan Blackmore
CONTEMPORARY ART Julian Stallabrass
CONTEMPORARY FICTION Robert Eaglestone
CONTINENTAL PHILOSOPHY Simon Critchley
COPERNICUS Owen Gingerich
CORAL REEFS Charles Sheppard
CORPORATE SOCIAL RESPONSIBILITY Jeremy Moon
CORRUPTION Leslie Holmes
COSMOLOGY Peter Coles
COUNTRY MUSIC Richard Carlin
CREATIVITY Vlad Glăveanu
CRIME FICTION Richard Bradford
CRIMINAL JUSTICE Julian V. Roberts
CRIMINOLOGY Tim Newburn
CRITICAL THEORY Stephen Eric Bronner
THE CRUSADES Christopher Tyerman
CRYPTOGRAPHY Fred Piper and Sean Murphy
CRYSTALLOGRAPHY A. M. Glazer
THE CULTURAL REVOLUTION Richard Curt Kraus
DADA AND SURREALISM David Hopkins
DANTE Peter Hainsworth and David Robey
DARWIN Jonathan Howard

THE DEAD SEA SCROLLS Timothy H. Lim
DECADENCE David Weir
DECOLONIZATION Dane Kennedy
DEMENTIA Kathleen Taylor
DEMOCRACY Bernard Crick
DEMOGRAPHY Sarah Harper
DEPRESSION Jan Scott and Mary Jane Tacchi
DERRIDA Simon Glendinning
DESCARTES Tom Sorell
DESERTS Nick Middleton
DESIGN John Heskett
DEVELOPMENT Ian Goldin
DEVELOPMENTAL BIOLOGY Lewis Wolpert
THE DEVIL Darren Oldridge
DIASPORA Kevin Kenny
CHARLES DICKENS Jenny Hartley
DICTIONARIES Lynda Mugglestone
DINOSAURS David Norman
DIPLOMATIC HISTORY Joseph M. Siracusa
DOCUMENTARY FILM Patricia Aufderheide
DREAMING J. Allan Hobson
DRUGS Les Iversen
DRUIDS Barry Cunliffe
DYNASTY Jeroen Duindam
DYSLEXIA Margaret J. Snowling
EARLY MUSIC Thomas Forrest Kelly
THE EARTH Martin Redfern
EARTH SYSTEM SCIENCE Tim Lenton
ECOLOGY Jaboury Ghazoul
ECONOMICS Partha Dasgupta
EDUCATION Gary Thomas
EGYPTIAN MYTH Geraldine Pinch
EIGHTEENTH-CENTURY BRITAIN Paul Langford
THE ELEMENTS Philip Ball
EMOTION Dylan Evans
EMPIRE Stephen Howe
EMPLOYMENT LAW David Cabrelli
ENERGY SYSTEMS Nick Jenkins
ENGELS Terrell Carver
ENGINEERING David Blockley
THE ENGLISH LANGUAGE Simon Horobin
ENGLISH LITERATURE Jonathan Bate
THE ENLIGHTENMENT John Robertson
ENTREPRENEURSHIP Paul Westhead and Mike Wright
ENVIRONMENTAL ECONOMICS Stephen Smith
ENVIRONMENTAL ETHICS Robin Attfield
ENVIRONMENTAL LAW Elizabeth Fisher
ENVIRONMENTAL POLITICS Andrew Dobson
ENZYMES Paul Engel
EPICUREANISM Catherine Wilson
EPIDEMIOLOGY Rodolfo Saracci
ETHICS Simon Blackburn
ETHNOMUSICOLOGY Timothy Rice
THE ETRUSCANS Christopher Smith
EUGENICS Philippa Levine
THE EUROPEAN UNION Simon Usherwood and John Pinder
EUROPEAN UNION LAW Anthony Arnull
EVANGELICALISM John G. Stackhouse Jr.
EVIL Luke Russell
EVOLUTION Brian and Deborah Charlesworth
EXISTENTIALISM Thomas Flynn
EXPLORATION Stewart A. Weaver
EXTINCTION Paul B. Wignall
THE EYE Michael Land
FAIRY TALE Marina Warner
FAMILY LAW Jonathan Herring
MICHAEL FARADAY Frank A. J. L. James
FASCISM Kevin Passmore
FASHION Rebecca Arnold
FEDERALISM Mark J. Rozell and Clyde Wilcox
FEMINISM Margaret Walters
FILM Michael Wood
FILM MUSIC Kathryn Kalinak
FILM NOIR James Naremore
FIRE Andrew C. Scott
THE FIRST WORLD WAR Michael Howard
FLUID MECHANICS Eric Lauga
FOLK MUSIC Mark Slobin
FOOD John Krebs

FORENSIC PSYCHOLOGY David Canter
FORENSIC SCIENCE Jim Fraser
FORESTS Jaboury Ghazoul
FOSSILS Keith Thomson
FOUCAULT Gary Gutting
THE FOUNDING FATHERS R. B. Bernstein
FRACTALS Kenneth Falconer
FREE SPEECH Nigel Warburton
FREE WILL Thomas Pink
FREEMASONRY Andreas Önnerfors
FRENCH LITERATURE John D. Lyons
FRENCH PHILOSOPHY Stephen Gaukroger and Knox Peden
THE FRENCH REVOLUTION William Doyle
FREUD Anthony Storr
FUNDAMENTALISM Malise Ruthven
FUNGI Nicholas P. Money
THE FUTURE Jennifer M. Gidley
GALAXIES John Gribbin
GALILEO Stillman Drake
GAME THEORY Ken Binmore
GANDHI Bhikhu Parekh
GARDEN HISTORY Gordon Campbell
GENES Jonathan Slack
GENIUS Andrew Robinson
GENOMICS John Archibald
GEOGRAPHY John Matthews and David Herbert
GEOLOGY Jan Zalasiewicz
GEOMETRY Maciej Dunajski
GEOPHYSICS William Lowrie
GEOPOLITICS Klaus Dodds
GERMAN LITERATURE Nicholas Boyle
GERMAN PHILOSOPHY Andrew Bowie
THE GHETTO Bryan Cheyette
GLACIATION David J. A. Evans
GLOBAL CATASTROPHES Bill McGuire
GLOBAL ECONOMIC HISTORY Robert C. Allen
GLOBAL ISLAM Nile Green
GLOBALIZATION Manfred B. Steger
GOD John Bowker
GÖDEL'S THEOREM A. W. Moore
GOETHE Ritchie Robertson
THE GOTHIC Nick Groom
GOVERNANCE Mark Bevir
GRAVITY Timothy Clifton
THE GREAT DEPRESSION AND THE NEW DEAL Eric Rauchway
HABEAS CORPUS Amanda L. Tyler
HABERMAS James Gordon Finlayson
THE HABSBURG EMPIRE Martyn Rady
HAPPINESS Daniel M. Haybron
THE HARLEM RENAISSANCE Cheryl A. Wall
THE HEBREW BIBLE AS LITERATURE Tod Linafelt
HEGEL Peter Singer
HEIDEGGER Michael Inwood
THE HELLENISTIC AGE Peter Thonemann
HEREDITY John Waller
HERMENEUTICS Jens Zimmermann
HERODOTUS Jennifer T. Roberts
HIEROGLYPHS Penelope Wilson
HINDUISM Kim Knott
HISTORY John H. Arnold
THE HISTORY OF ASTRONOMY Michael Hoskin
THE HISTORY OF CHEMISTRY William H. Brock
THE HISTORY OF CHILDHOOD James Marten
THE HISTORY OF CINEMA Geoffrey Nowell-Smith
THE HISTORY OF COMPUTING Doron Swade
THE HISTORY OF LIFE Michael Benton
THE HISTORY OF MATHEMATICS Jacqueline Stedall
THE HISTORY OF MEDICINE William Bynum
THE HISTORY OF PHYSICS J. L. Heilbron
THE HISTORY OF POLITICAL THOUGHT Richard Whatmore
THE HISTORY OF TIME Leofranc Holford-Strevens
HIV AND AIDS Alan Whiteside
HOBBES Richard Tuck
HOLLYWOOD Peter Decherney
THE HOLY ROMAN EMPIRE Joachim Whaley
HOME Michael Allen Fox
HOMER Barbara Graziosi

HORMONES Martin Luck
HORROR Darryl Jones
HUMAN ANATOMY Leslie Klenerman
HUMAN EVOLUTION Bernard Wood
HUMAN PHYSIOLOGY
Jamie A. Davies
HUMAN RESOURCE
MANAGEMENT Adrian Wilkinson
HUMAN RIGHTS Andrew Clapham
HUMANISM Stephen Law
HUME James A. Harris
HUMOUR Noël Carroll
THE ICE AGE Jamie Woodward
IDENTITY Florian Coulmas
IDEOLOGY Michael Freeden
THE IMMUNE SYSTEM
Paul Klenerman
INDIAN CINEMA Ashish Rajadhyaksha
INDIAN PHILOSOPHY Sue Hamilton
THE INDUSTRIAL REVOLUTION
Robert C. Allen
INFECTIOUS DISEASE Marta L. Wayne and Benjamin M. Bolker
INFINITY Ian Stewart
INFORMATION Luciano Floridi
INNOVATION Mark Dodgson and David Gann
INTELLECTUAL PROPERTY
Siva Vaidhyanathan
INTELLIGENCE Ian J. Deary
INTERNATIONAL LAW
Vaughan Lowe
INTERNATIONAL MIGRATION
Khalid Koser
INTERNATIONAL RELATIONS
Christian Reus-Smit
INTERNATIONAL SECURITY
Christopher S. Browning
INSECTS Simon Leather
IRAN Ali M. Ansari
ISLAM Malise Ruthven
ISLAMIC HISTORY Adam Silverstein
ISLAMIC LAW Mashood A. Baderin
ISOTOPES Rob Ellam
ITALIAN LITERATURE
Peter Hainsworth and David Robey
HENRY JAMES Susan L. Mizruchi
JESUS Richard Bauckham
JEWISH HISTORY David N. Myers
JEWISH LITERATURE Ilan Stavans
JOURNALISM Ian Hargreaves
JAMES JOYCE Colin MacCabe
JUDAISM Norman Solomon
JUNG Anthony Stevens
KABBALAH Joseph Dan
KAFKA Ritchie Robertson
KANT Roger Scruton
KEYNES Robert Skidelsky
KIERKEGAARD Patrick Gardiner
KNOWLEDGE Jennifer Nagel
THE KORAN Michael Cook
KOREA Michael J. Seth
LAKES Warwick F. Vincent
LANDSCAPE ARCHITECTURE
Ian H. Thompson
LANDSCAPES AND GEOMORPHOLOGY
Andrew Goudie and Heather Viles
LANGUAGES Stephen R. Anderson
LATE ANTIQUITY Gillian Clark
LAW Raymond Wacks
THE LAWS OF THERMODYNAMICS
Peter Atkins
LEADERSHIP Keith Grint
LEARNING Mark Haselgrove
LEIBNIZ Maria Rosa Antognazza
C. S. LEWIS James Como
LIBERALISM Michael Freeden
LIGHT Ian Walmsley
LINCOLN Allen C. Guelzo
LINGUISTICS Peter Matthews
LITERARY THEORY Jonathan Culler
LOCKE John Dunn
LOGIC Graham Priest
LOVE Ronald de Sousa
MARTIN LUTHER Scott H. Hendrix
MACHIAVELLI Quentin Skinner
MADNESS Andrew Scull
MAGIC Owen Davies
MAGNA CARTA Nicholas Vincent
MAGNETISM Stephen Blundell
MALTHUS Donald Winch
MAMMALS T. S. Kemp
MANAGEMENT John Hendry
NELSON MANDELA Elleke Boehmer
MAO Delia Davin
MARINE BIOLOGY Philip V. Mladenov
MARKETING
Kenneth Le Meunier-FitzHugh
THE MARQUIS DE SADE John Phillips

MARTYRDOM Jolyon Mitchell
MARX Peter Singer
MATERIALS Christopher Hall
MATHEMATICAL FINANCE
Mark H. A. Davis
MATHEMATICS Timothy Gowers
MATTER Geoff Cottrell
THE MAYA Matthew Restall and
Amara Solari
THE MEANING OF LIFE
Terry Eagleton
MEASUREMENT David Hand
MEDICAL ETHICS
Michael Dunn and Tony Hope
MEDICAL LAW Charles Foster
MEDIEVAL BRITAIN
John Gillingham and Ralph A. Griffiths
MEDIEVAL LITERATURE
Elaine Treharne
MEDIEVAL PHILOSOPHY
John Marenbon
MEMORY Jonathan K. Foster
METAPHYSICS Stephen Mumford
METHODISM William J. Abraham
THE MEXICAN REVOLUTION
Alan Knight
MICROBIOLOGY Nicholas P. Money
MICROBIOMES Angela E. Douglas
MICROECONOMICS Avinash Dixit
MICROSCOPY Terence Allen
THE MIDDLE AGES Miri Rubin
MILITARY JUSTICE
Eugene R. Fidell
MILITARY STRATEGY
Antulio J. Echevarria II
JOHN STUART MILL Gregory Claeys
MINERALS David Vaughan
MIRACLES Yujin Nagasawa
MODERN ARCHITECTURE
Adam Sharr
MODERN ART David Cottington
MODERN BRAZIL Anthony W. Pereira
MODERN CHINA Rana Mitter
MODERN DRAMA
Kirsten E. Shepherd-Barr
MODERN FRANCE
Vanessa R. Schwartz
MODERN INDIA Craig Jeffrey
MODERN IRELAND Senia Pašeta
MODERN ITALY Anna Cento Bull
MODERN JAPAN
Christopher Goto-Jones
MODERN LATIN AMERICAN
LITERATURE
Roberto González Echevarría
MODERN WAR Richard English
MODERNISM Christopher Butler
MOLECULAR BIOLOGY Aysha Divan
and Janice A. Royds
MOLECULES Philip Ball
MONASTICISM Stephen J. Davis
THE MONGOLS Morris Rossabi
MONTAIGNE William M. Hamlin
MOONS David A. Rothery
MORMONISM Richard Lyman Bushman
MOUNTAINS Martin F. Price
MUHAMMAD Jonathan A. C. Brown
MULTICULTURALISM Ali Rattansi
MULTILINGUALISM John C. Maher
MUSIC Nicholas Cook
MUSIC AND TECHNOLOGY
Mark Katz
MYTH Robert A. Segal
NANOTECHNOLOGY Philip Moriarty
NAPOLEON David A. Bell
THE NAPOLEONIC WARS
Mike Rapport
NATIONALISM Steven Grosby
NATIVE AMERICAN LITERATURE
Sean Teuton
NAVIGATION Jim Bennett
NAZI GERMANY Jane Caplan
NEGOTIATION Carrie Menkel-Meadow
NEOLIBERALISM Manfred B. Steger
and Ravi K. Roy
NETWORKS Guido Caldarelli and
Michele Catanzaro
THE NEW TESTAMENT
Luke Timothy Johnson
THE NEW TESTAMENT AS
LITERATURE Kyle Keefer
NEWTON Robert Iliffe
NIETZSCHE Michael Tanner
NINETEENTH-CENTURY
BRITAIN Christopher Harvie and
H. C. G. Matthew
THE NORMAN CONQUEST
George Garnett

NORTH AMERICAN INDIANS Theda Perdue and Michael D. Green
NORTHERN IRELAND Marc Mulholland
NOTHING Frank Close
NUCLEAR PHYSICS Frank Close
NUCLEAR POWER Maxwell Irvine
NUCLEAR WEAPONS Joseph M. Siracusa
NUMBER THEORY Robin Wilson
NUMBERS Peter M. Higgins
NUTRITION David A. Bender
OBJECTIVITY Stephen Gaukroger
OCEANS Dorrik Stow
THE OLD TESTAMENT Michael D. Coogan
THE ORCHESTRA D. Kern Holoman
ORGANIC CHEMISTRY Graham Patrick
ORGANIZATIONS Mary Jo Hatch
ORGANIZED CRIME Georgios A. Antonopoulos and Georgios Papanicolaou
ORTHODOX CHRISTIANITY A. Edward Siecienski
OVID Llewelyn Morgan
PAGANISM Owen Davies
PAKISTAN Pippa Virdee
THE PALESTINIAN-ISRAELI CONFLICT Martin Bunton
PANDEMICS Christian W. McMillen
PARTICLE PHYSICS Frank Close
PAUL E. P. Sanders
IVAN PAVLOV Daniel P. Todes
PEACE Oliver P. Richmond
PENTECOSTALISM William K. Kay
PERCEPTION Brian Rogers
THE PERIODIC TABLE Eric R. Scerri
PHILOSOPHICAL METHOD Timothy Williamson
PHILOSOPHY Edward Craig
PHILOSOPHY IN THE ISLAMIC WORLD Peter Adamson
PHILOSOPHY OF BIOLOGY Samir Okasha
PHILOSOPHY OF LAW Raymond Wacks
PHILOSOPHY OF MIND Barbara Gail Montero
PHILOSOPHY OF PHYSICS David Wallace
PHILOSOPHY OF SCIENCE Samir Okasha
PHILOSOPHY OF RELIGION Tim Bayne
PHOTOGRAPHY Steve Edwards
PHYSICAL CHEMISTRY Peter Atkins
PHYSICS Sidney Perkowitz
PILGRIMAGE Ian Reader
PLAGUE Paul Slack
PLANETARY SYSTEMS Raymond T. Pierrehumbert
PLANETS David A. Rothery
PLANTS Timothy Walker
PLATE TECTONICS Peter Molnar
PLATO Julia Annas
POETRY Bernard O'Donoghue
POLITICAL PHILOSOPHY David Miller
POLITICS Kenneth Minogue
POLYGAMY Sarah M. S. Pearsall
POPULISM Cas Mudde and Cristóbal Rovira Kaltwasser
POSTCOLONIALISM Robert J. C. Young
POSTMODERNISM Christopher Butler
POSTSTRUCTURALISM Catherine Belsey
POVERTY Philip N. Jefferson
PREHISTORY Chris Gosden
PRESOCRATIC PHILOSOPHY Catherine Osborne
PRIVACY Raymond Wacks
PROBABILITY John Haigh
PROGRESSIVISM Walter Nugent
PROHIBITION W. J. Rorabaugh
PROJECTS Andrew Davies
PROTESTANTISM Mark A. Noll
PSYCHIATRY Tom Burns
PSYCHOANALYSIS Daniel Pick
PSYCHOLOGY Gillian Butler and Freda McManus
PSYCHOLOGY OF MUSIC Elizabeth Hellmuth Margulis
PSYCHOPATHY Essi Viding
PSYCHOTHERAPY Tom Burns and Eva Burns-Lundgren
PUBLIC ADMINISTRATION Stella Z. Theodoulou and Ravi K. Roy

PUBLIC HEALTH Virginia Berridge
PURITANISM Francis J. Bremer
THE QUAKERS Pink Dandelion
QUANTUM THEORY John Polkinghorne
RACISM Ali Rattansi
RADIOACTIVITY Claudio Tuniz
RASTAFARI Ennis B. Edmonds
READING Belinda Jack
THE REAGAN REVOLUTION Gil Troy
REALITY Jan Westerhoff
RECONSTRUCTION Allen C. Guelzo
THE REFORMATION Peter Marshall
REFUGEES Gil Loescher
RELATIVITY Russell Stannard
RELIGION Thomas A. Tweed
RELIGION IN AMERICA Timothy Beal
THE RENAISSANCE Jerry Brotton
RENAISSANCE ART Geraldine A. Johnson
RENEWABLE ENERGY Nick Jelley
REPTILES T. S. Kemp
REVOLUTIONS Jack A. Goldstone
RHETORIC Richard Toye
RISK Baruch Fischhoff and John Kadvany
RITUAL Barry Stephenson
RIVERS Nick Middleton
ROBOTICS Alan Winfield
ROCKS Jan Zalasiewicz
ROMAN BRITAIN Peter Salway
THE ROMAN EMPIRE Christopher Kelly
THE ROMAN REPUBLIC David M. Gwynn
ROMANTICISM Michael Ferber
ROUSSEAU Robert Wokler
RUSSELL A. C. Grayling
THE RUSSIAN ECONOMY Richard Connolly
RUSSIAN HISTORY Geoffrey Hosking
RUSSIAN LITERATURE Catriona Kelly
THE RUSSIAN REVOLUTION S. A. Smith
SAINTS Simon Yarrow
SAMURAI Michael Wert
SAVANNAS Peter A. Furley
SCEPTICISM Duncan Pritchard
SCHIZOPHRENIA Chris Frith and Eve Johnstone
SCHOPENHAUER Christopher Janaway
SCIENCE AND RELIGION Thomas Dixon and Adam R. Shapiro
SCIENCE FICTION David Seed
THE SCIENTIFIC REVOLUTION Lawrence M. Principe
SCOTLAND Rab Houston
SECULARISM Andrew Copson
SEXUAL SELECTION Marlene Zuk and Leigh W. Simmons
SEXUALITY Véronique Mottier
WILLIAM SHAKESPEARE Stanley Wells
SHAKESPEARE'S COMEDIES Bart van Es
SHAKESPEARE'S SONNETS AND POEMS Jonathan F. S. Post
SHAKESPEARE'S TRAGEDIES Stanley Wells
GEORGE BERNARD SHAW Christopher Wixson
MARY SHELLEY Charlotte Gordon
THE SHORT STORY Andrew Kahn
SIKHISM Eleanor Nesbitt
SILENT FILM Donna Kornhaber
THE SILK ROAD James A. Millward
SLANG Jonathon Green
SLEEP Steven W. Lockley and Russell G. Foster
SMELL Matthew Cobb
ADAM SMITH Christopher J. Berry
SOCIAL AND CULTURAL ANTHROPOLOGY John Monaghan and Peter Just
SOCIAL PSYCHOLOGY Richard J. Crisp
SOCIAL WORK Sally Holland and Jonathan Scourfield
SOCIALISM Michael Newman
SOCIOLINGUISTICS John Edwards
SOCIOLOGY Steve Bruce
SOCRATES C. C. W. Taylor
SOFT MATTER Tom McLeish
SOUND Mike Goldsmith
SOUTHEAST ASIA James R. Rush
THE SOVIET UNION Stephen Lovell
THE SPANISH CIVIL WAR Helen Graham

SPANISH LITERATURE Jo Labanyi
THE SPARTANS Andrew J. Bayliss
SPINOZA Roger Scruton
SPIRITUALITY Philip Sheldrake
SPORT Mike Cronin
STARS Andrew King
STATISTICS David J. Hand
STEM CELLS Jonathan Slack
STOICISM Brad Inwood
STRUCTURAL ENGINEERING David Blockley
STUART BRITAIN John Morrill
THE SUN Philip Judge
SUPERCONDUCTIVITY Stephen Blundell
SUPERSTITION Stuart Vyse
SYMMETRY Ian Stewart
SYNAESTHESIA Julia Simner
SYNTHETIC BIOLOGY Jamie A. Davies
SYSTEMS BIOLOGY Eberhard O. Voit
TAXATION Stephen Smith
TEETH Peter S. Ungar
TELESCOPES Geoff Cottrell
TERRORISM Charles Townshend
THEATRE Marvin Carlson
THEOLOGY David F. Ford
THINKING AND REASONING Jonathan St B. T. Evans
THOUGHT Tim Bayne
TIBETAN BUDDHISM Matthew T. Kapstein
TIDES David George Bowers and Emyr Martyn Roberts
TIME Jenann Ismael
TOCQUEVILLE Harvey C. Mansfield
LEO TOLSTOY Liza Knapp
TOPOLOGY Richard Earl
TRAGEDY Adrian Poole
TRANSLATION Matthew Reynolds
THE TREATY OF VERSAILLES Michael S. Neiberg
TRIGONOMETRY Glen Van Brummelen
THE TROJAN WAR Eric H. Cline
TRUST Katherine Hawley
THE TUDORS John Guy
TWENTIETH-CENTURY BRITAIN Kenneth O. Morgan
TYPOGRAPHY Paul Luna
THE UNITED NATIONS Jussi M. Hanhimäki
UNIVERSITIES AND COLLEGES David Palfreyman and Paul Temple
THE U.S. CIVIL WAR Louis P. Masur
THE U.S. CONGRESS Donald A. Ritchie
THE U.S. CONSTITUTION David J. Bodenhamer
THE U.S. SUPREME COURT Linda Greenhouse
UTILITARIANISM Katarzyna de Lazari-Radek and Peter Singer
UTOPIANISM Lyman Tower Sargent
VATICAN II Shaun Blanchard and Stephen Bullivant
VETERINARY SCIENCE James Yeates
THE VIKINGS Julian D. Richards
VIOLENCE Philip Dwyer
THE VIRGIN MARY Mary Joan Winn Leith
THE VIRTUES Craig A. Boyd and Kevin Timpe
VIRUSES Dorothy H. Crawford
VOLCANOES Michael J. Branney and Jan Zalasiewicz
VOLTAIRE Nicholas Cronk
WAR AND RELIGION Jolyon Mitchell and Joshua Rey
WAR AND TECHNOLOGY Alex Roland
WATER John Finney
WAVES Mike Goldsmith
WEATHER Storm Dunlop
THE WELFARE STATE David Garland
WITCHCRAFT Malcolm Gaskill
WITTGENSTEIN A. C. Grayling
WORK Stephen Fineman
WORLD MUSIC Philip Bohlman
WORLD MYTHOLOGY David Leeming
THE WORLD TRADE ORGANIZATION Amrita Narlikar
WORLD WAR II Gerhard L. Weinberg
WRITING AND SCRIPT Andrew Robinson
ZIONISM Michael Stanislawski
ÉMILE ZOLA Brian Nelson

Available soon:

OBSERVATIONAL ASTRONOMY
Geoff Cottrell
MATHEMATICAL ANALYSIS
Richard Earl
HISTORY OF EMOTIONS
Thomas Dixon

Shaun Blanchard and Stephen Bullivant

VATICAN II

A Very Short Introduction

OXFORD
UNIVERSITY PRESS

Great Clarendon Street, Oxford, OX2 6DP,
United Kingdom

Oxford University Press is a department of the University of Oxford.
It furthers the University's objective of excellence in research, scholarship,
and education by publishing worldwide. Oxford is a registered trade mark of
Oxford University Press in the UK and in certain other countries

First edition published in 2023

Published in the United States of America by Oxford University Press
198 Madison Avenue, New York, NY 10016, United States of America

British Library Cataloguing in Publication Data
Data available

Library of Congress Control Number: 2022944961

ISBN 978-0-19-886481-3

Printed and bound by
CPI Group (UK) Ltd, Croydon, CR0 4YY

Contents

Acknowledgements

Shaun Blanchard: As someone born in 1986, the reception of Vatican II has marked my life as a Catholic and as a young academic. I am indebted to two wonderful men for first sparking my interest in the Council. The first is Monsignor John Wall, a priest of the Diocese of Raleigh (North Carolina). Fr Wall was a seminarian at the North American College in Rome in the lead-up to Vatican II and attended John XXIII's coronation in 1958. As an undergrad with a keen interest in history and theology, Fr Wall's stories of meeting John XXIII, of the shock of the liturgical changes, and of the excitement of the conciliar event and aftermath made a deep impression upon me. The second formative figure is Dr Yaakov Ariel, who guided me through a project on *Nostra Aetate* and Jewish–Catholic dialogue for my senior seminar at the University of North Carolina. Discovering Vatican II as a historical event in all its depth and richness—rather than as an ideological symbol bent to demonization or uncritical lionization—opened up a much larger world for me.

In my postgraduate study at Oxford and Marquette, I am indebted to Johannes Zachhuber, Fr Philip Endean, SJ, the Dominicans at Blackfriars Hall, Fr David Schultenover, SJ, Susan Wood, Fr Joseph Mueller, SJ, and Ulrich Lehner. I greatly benefited from a graduate seminar with Dr Wood, in which I first explored the Alberigo volumes and classic commentaries like Vorgrimler's.

It is with Fr Mueller that I first delved into the conciliar *Acta* in a project on Vatican II ecclesiology and the 'ghosts' of the past. This work marked my dissertation, first monograph, and subsequent research. I wish also to thank Kristin Colberg, John Stayne, Paul Murray, Lewis Ayres, Massimo Faggioli, Matthew Levering, Gavin D'Costa, John Meinert, Andrew and Julia Meszaros, and the many others with whom I have had engaging conversations, debates, and exchanges regarding Vatican II. Colleagues at the National Institute for Newman Studies—especially Kenneth Parker, Elizabeth Huddleston, and Chris Cimorelli—have been engaging dialogue partners on Vatican II. I also thank the Institute for supporting my research.

I am, as ever, grateful to my wife Ann-Marie, for supporting me in innumerable ways and for inspiring me with her love of literature and the written word. To Stephen Bullivant: though COVID prevented us from haunting Oxfordshire pubs together, I am incredibly grateful for your wit and erudition throughout this project.

It is to the unfailingly patient, kind, and joyful Monsignor John Wall—a priest truly in the tradition of John XXIII—that I dedicate my work on this book.

Stephen Bullivant: My own 'history' with Vatican II parallels, in some measure, my co-author's. I first discovered the Council, and indeed the whole 'golden generation' of Catholic theologians—Congar, Rahner, De Lubac, Daniélou, Chenu, Ratzinger—who helped to ghost write it, as an undergraduate, and was sufficiently intrigued to then devote three years of doctoral work to wrestling with two sentences of *Lumen Gentium*. Since then, even when not working directly on the Council itself (or, as I have more recently, on its reception and consequences), its influence has been hard to escape. I have also taught the Council to undergrads and postgrads of my own—two of whom, I'm proud to say, have ended up being cited in this volume's bibliography in their own right.

While the various debts I've incurred over the years are far too many to recall, those who certainly do warrant a mention for having helped, in some significant way, towards my writing of this book include: Gavin D'Costa, Gregory Murphy OP, Joseph Bailham OP, Joseph Shaw, John Dickson, Philip Kennedy OP, Philip Endean SJ, Alcuin Reid OSB, Hugh Somerville Knapman OSB, Karen Kilby, Patricia Kelly, Wilfrid Jones, and Matthew Levering.

As ever, all our dealings with those at OUP have been a delight. Special thanks go to Andrea Keegan, Christina Fleischer, Jenny Nugee, and Luciana O'Flaherty—without whom, in a very literal sense, this book would not exist.

Working with Shaun, a friend of many years, has been a joy from start to finish. Though I too am sad that, while we wrote much of the original book proposal together at my local Wetherspoon's pub, the subsequent pandemic prevented the book itself from being produced in so genteel a manner.

Throughout the whole process, my wife Joanna and our children have been as delightful as ever. Particular mention is due to little Leo Joseph, who arrived just in time to provide ample opportunity for much Cardinal Suenens-related humour in the final months of writing. It is to little Leo that I dedicate my own share of this work.

List of illustrations

Note on sources

Formal teaching documents of the Catholic Church typically have two titles. The shortest and most commonly used is simply taken from the text's opening two or three words, which are usually in Latin. (Because Latin word order is flexible, it is possible to move meaningful phrases to the start of sentences. Hence the Latin shorthand title normally intimates something of the 'flavour' of the document.) The second is a longer and more descriptive one, explaining the specific type of document and its general subject matter. Hence the Second Vatican Council's document *Lumen Gentium* ('Light of the nations') is also called 'The Dogmatic Constitution on the Church'. When citing specific passages, we will typically give the Latin 'shorthand' title in full, followed by the relevant paragraph or clause number: for example, '*Lumen Gentium* 16'. For subsequent citations within quick succession we use an abbreviation in the format 'LG 22'. For ease of reference, we give a full list of the Council's sixteen main documents, with both titles, in an Appendix.

Quotations from formal church documents are, where available, given according to the 'official' English translations, readily available on the Vatican's own website (www.vatican.va), though we have occasionally amended these slightly.

Where we have quoted or mentioned other sources, full details are provided in the relevant chapter's section of the References and Further Reading.

Chapter 1
What is an 'ecumenical council'?

The Second Vatican Council (1962–5), or Vatican II, is the most significant episode in the life of the Catholic Church over the past century. A plausible case can, moreover, be made for it being among the most significant happenings within global religious history of the past 500 years. There are two main reasons for this. In the first place, with over a billion members, the Catholic Church is the largest denomination of Christianity, which is in turn the world's biggest religion. As we shall see in the following chapters, Vatican II initiated profound changes—some intentionally, others less so—both at the 'high' levels of church teaching and governance, and in the concrete religious, moral, and social lives of all these ordinary believers. In the second place, the Council substantially reconfigured, intellectually and practically, the Church's relationships with those outside it. This is true most obviously, though far from exclusively, with regard to the Jews and members of other Christian denominations. Vatican II was not only of interest or importance for Catholics themselves. In fact, and to a degree that might today seem strange, a large number of non-Catholic groups—religious bodies, NGOs, governments, the world's media—took keen (and often vested) interests in its progress and proceedings. Many cared enough about the Council's doings to try, in various invited and uninvited ways, to influence what and how it did them.

1. Cartoon by John Ryan, published in *The Catholic Herald*, 1962.

The purpose of this short book is hence to explain three things about Vatican II: what it was, why it mattered, and why—over 50 years later—it still does. This is no easy task. The official Latin 'Acts' of the Council alone take up several shelves of heavy volumes. Even during the few years it was in session the thousands of participants collectively produced vast troves of diaries, letters, talks, commentaries, and even comic verse, all of which can help shed light on the whole affair (including, in the latter case, on just how bored some of the participants got during the debates). Naturally, after the Council, many of them (have) spent much of the rest of their lives interpreting, implementing, arguing over, or otherwise reminiscing about what they often regarded as—in the words of Cardinal König of Vienna, but echoed more or less verbatim by many others—'the highlight of my life'. And of course, all these 'primary sources' have themselves spawned a vast, multilingual, and ever-growing secondary literature, touching on seemingly all aspects of Vatican II's history, teaching, and reception. (To give some idea of this: one of the current authors published a 90,000-word book, devoted to explicating just two sentences [!] of *Lumen Gentium.*)

In the interests of space, we have generally avoided giving extensive quotations from the conciliar texts themselves (these are widely and easily available, not least online), or from secondary sources (though those we have principally drawn on are listed in the References and Further Reading). We have, though, been sure to make room for various 'voices' from those who were *there* in various capacities. We hope these give at least a small sense of the multiplicity of ways in which Vatican II was seen, felt, and understood, both during and after the event itself.

This book is divided into seven further chapters. Chapter 2 explains how the Council came to be, in terms of both its proximate causes (i.e. the when, why, and how of its calling), and the backstory of various currents of Catholic theology and history which flowed, if in some cases rather meanderingly, into it. Chapter 3 provides a potted history of Vatican II: the main contours of how the event itself actually played out over, and between, the four sessions.

The following four chapters focus on what the Council actually taught and enacted. Naturally prominent here will be the 16 principal documents it produced. We will particularly focus on the four which the Council itself deemed the most important—that is, the four 'Constitutions'—while considering aspects of various other 'Decrees' and 'Declarations', which tend to be shorter and more focused on giving an in-depth treatment of a specific topic, in light of them.

In all four of these chapters, our primary aims are to introduce the key ideas in the texts themselves, and to explain something of how they came to be there. Where possible, we will also explore—or at least point readers to where others have explored—aspects of how the conciliar teachings have fared once 'released into the wild'.

While this is itself an enormous topic, and we will therefore have to be very selective, it is also critical. For the Council's teachings were always intended to be received and implemented far beyond the printed page: the Council Fathers, as the Jesuit historian John O'Malley has rightly emphasized, '*wanted* something to happen'. What somethings actually did then happen, even if not always the somethings that were hoped to, are thus indispensable parts of the Council's story and ongoing relevance.

They are also critical for comprehending why Vatican II has been, and still is, the source of much controversy and contestation. This will be the subject of the eighth and final chapter, which looks at the overall legacy of the Council, and the various main ways of interpreting and making sense of it all ('hermeneutics') which have emerged in the half-century-and-more since it closed.

'Ecumenical council'?

The significance of Vatican II flows, in multiple ways, from its status as an 'ecumenical council'—indeed, as the 21st such one in the history of the Catholic Church. But what, precisely, *is* an 'ecumenical council' in the first place? One cannot properly grasp why *this* particular Council matters, without a basic sense of the (Catholic) meaning of an 'ecumenical council', and the special authority that such gatherings are considered to possess.

According to the *Code of Canon Law* (the systematic revision of which, completed in 1983, was itself one of the late-flowering fruits of Vatican II), an ecumenical council is a special gathering of the world's bishops, mandated by the pope, in order that they might collectively 'exercise power over the universal Church in a solemn manner'. That's a start, at least.

'Bishops' here, of course, means *Catholic* bishops, which in practice means those of the Latin Church, or of one of the 23 Eastern Catholic Churches in full communion with the pope (the bishop of Rome). This is important to note since, contrary to popular perception (not least among Catholics themselves), 'the Catholic Church' strictly speaking comprises a couple of dozen 'particular Church*es*', each with their own hierarchies, customs, practices, liturgical rites, and ways of doing things. The Latin Church is the largest of these, and thanks to the traditional primacy of Rome, has tended to overshadow the others, though all are of 'equal dignity' (*Orientalium Ecclesiarum* 3). This was something many Eastern Catholic bishops felt keen to stress during the Council itself. (Hence Patriarch Maximos IV Saigh, head of the Melkite Greek Catholic Church, symbolically refusing to speak in Latin—the traditional lingua franca of the Latin particular Church, not the Catholic Church itself—during debates. He spoke French instead.)

There is, therefore, a certain sense in which Vatican II was an *ecumenical* council in something like the modern meaning of the term—since the Catholic Church is, in itself, an ecumenical confederation of ('particular') churches. It was also ecumenical in the more usual senses of seeking to build better relationships with other, non-Catholic Christian communities, with the ultimate long-term, if (so far) elusive, hope of achieving formal unity with some of them.

Confusingly, that is not what the word really means in the phrase 'ecumenical council'. Rather, its root comes from the Greek word *oikumene*, meaning the known or inhabited world. Ecumenical, in this sense, is therefore intended (a little poetically) to convey the idea of *all* the bishops coming together from the ends of the earth for a special purpose. In practice, actual ecumenical councils have never managed to live up to that aspiration. The first of them, held at Nicaea (modern-day Turkey) in 325, was near-exclusively an Eastern affair—though the Western half of the Empire's bishops were represented in the person of Hosius of Cordoba, who presided over the Council, and the bishop of Rome gave it his blessing. Some sessions of the 19th Council, held at Trent in Italy from 1545 to 1563 (on and off!), had only a few dozen bishops present. But the *idea* of an ecumenical council as a gathering of all the bishops nonetheless endured, albeit accompanied with realistic expectations as to what that might actually amount to. In fact, only with Vatican I and—to a vastly greater extent—Vatican II has anything like this ideal been practicably achievable, thanks to modern transportation. For the former, held in 1869–70 and attended by over 700 bishops, some of the more far-flung had to travel for weeks by foot, horse, ship, and train to be there. For the latter, attended by well over 2,000, it took the Archbishop of Adelaide a mere 27½ hours to fly in from Australia. Not even Vatican II could boast the full episcopal *oikumene*, however. Some bishops had to stay away for age or health reasons, of course; others, not least from several communist countries, were actively *kept* away for political reasons.

Why, though, go to the considerable hassle and expense of bringing bishops together? The basic idea goes back to the early years of Christianity. Already in the New Testament we see disputes springing up either within, or between, local church communities, and one or more of the apostles being asked—or feeling at liberty—to adjudicate or intervene. This happens, most obviously, in several of Paul's letters (1 Corinthians 8:1–13, on the admissibility of eating meat sacrificed to idols, is a good example here). As time went on, and the first generation of apostles died off, we can trace how this basic role was then passed on to those whom these apostles had appointed as 'overseers' (*episkopoi*) of their communities—these were, in a literal sense 'the Successors of the Apostles'. This was not the only possible solution to the emerging problem of religious authority, and no doubt the system could (and still does) create troubles of its own. But this basic model seems to have been well established by the early 2nd century, at least in certain places (e.g. Antioch and Smyrna). Later that century, moreover, we see this doctrine of 'apostolic succession'—that is, the authority of the original apostles having been passed on to their successors, who have then passed it onto their successors, and so on—being cited as a safeguard against errors. St Irenaeus of Lyons, notably, cites the lineage of Rome's bishops leading back to Peter and Paul as a particularly clear example, though he is likewise confident that similar accounts can be given 'for the successions of all the Churches'.

Irenaeus' proposal is neat. Furthermore, his highlighting of Rome, plus his own genuinely East–West credentials (though he ended up as bishop of Lyons in France, he hailed from Asia Minor), have long made him a favourite of Catholic theologians of the episcopacy. What Irenaeus seems not to have foreseen, however, is the possibility that different Successors of the Apostles might fundamentally disagree over major issues. When this occasionally did happen, there was an equally neat solution—one also with a useful scriptural precedent (see Acts 15). The bishops of the area(s) in question would gather together and, ideally, either reach an amicable consensus or agree to disagree. If no such happy conclusion was possible then, if required, one view might carry the day, with those not accepting it condemned accordingly. Not surprisingly, this could in turn result in rival gatherings of like-minded bishops mutually condemning each other.

In fact, such councils or synods, in the sense of deliberative meetings of bishops, were fairly common in the Church's first few centuries. Some were 'extraordinary' meetings, called to settle particular disputes. Most though were regular affairs, presumably concerned with humdrum administrative matters (a good analogue here would be the regular plenary meetings of national bishops' conferences, encouraged by Vatican II). In the early decades of the 4th century, however, what *began* as a local dispute in Alexandria over the true nature of Jesus Christ soon spiralled out of control. Bishops throughout the whole Eastern half of the Roman Empire were soon being recruited by one side or the other. As the controversy deepened, the new Emperor Constantine was keen for the matter to be settled once and for all. Evidently, no local or regional council would be sufficiently definitive enough—all the usual mechanisms had been tried and failed. Instead, what was needed was a truly universal council, to which all the bishops of the whole *oikumene* would be invited...

Hence, of course, the very first ecumenical council, called to resolve the Arian crisis. That it didn't succeed in resolving the crisis, but arguably inflamed it, and required a *second* ecumenical council—at Constantinople in 381—actually to do so, is a fact that is sometimes missed. Nevertheless, the idea was set. Henceforth, ecumenical councils would be convened on an ad hoc basis, in order to meet some special crisis. Sometimes they might come in quick succession, as with the record seven—Lateran I–IV, Lyon I and II, and Vienne—which occurred between 1123 and 1312. Or else centuries might pass between one and the next, as with the over 300 years separating Trent and Vatican I. Averaging out at one every 90 years or so, ecumenical councils certainly count as exceptional events in the life of the Church. They are not things to be convoked lightly, which often means that when they *are*, things have already got well out of hand. (Nicaea is a good example here. So too is Trent, which opened 28 years after Luther published his *Ninety-Five Theses*.) History shows, moreover, how they can sometimes take on a life of their own. The conciliar path is rarely straight or smooth.

All of this begs an obvious question. What special crisis was Vatican II called to resolve? It is sometimes said here that the Council marked a new departure in conciliar history, because it was proactive rather than reactive; positive not negative; *for* things rather than called to oppose them. This claim gains credibility from the fact that the Council was careful not to issue formal anathemas. (Though we shall see in Chapter 7 that, as with so many generalizations about Vatican II, this statement needs a little qualification.) That is not quite the same as there not being any crisis at all, however.

So there was to be a second Vatican Council. What would be its business? Nothing in particular, it would appear; or perhaps it would be truer to say: everything.

Christopher Butler OSB, writing in 1966

Abbot-President of the English Benedictine Congregation, 1961–6; later auxiliary bishop of Westminster, England

It is easy to forget, perhaps, just how swiftly after the Second World War—and with it the Holocaust, the atomic bombings of Japan, and myriad other horrors—the Council followed. Vatican II opened just 17 years after VE Day. Furthermore, since the 1930s in France, and soon after the war in countries such as Germany, Italy, and Belgium, priests and theologians had been worrying openly about the rapidly rising tide of de-Christianization in the heart of Christendom. Special concerns were expressed about the young and working classes, to whom it was felt the Church was becoming increasingly irrelevant, and a good deal of pastoral, liturgical, and evangelistic experimentation was already in the air (most famously with the French 'worker-priest' experiments, which saw clergy taking up jobs in factories, coalmines, and dockyards in order to 'win back' those distant from the Church, and show its relevance to contemporary social issues). Among those troubled by the rising tide of indifference and unbelief were priests and bishops such as Yves Congar, Henri de Lubac, Karl Rahner, Joseph Ratzinger, Angelo Roncalli, and Giovanni Montini—all of whom we'll be meeting again in these pages.

After the Council, these kinds of impulses would ultimately come to be termed 'the new evangelization', and be cited as an important fruit *of* it. But the basic issues, along with a felt need to address them, were well recognized beforehand. These are not the only factors that can plausibly be cited as preparing the way for a

Council, and we will identify several other likely motivators in the next chapter. But this widespread sense of a nascent pastoral crisis—that, as theologian Karl Rahner wrote in 1954, 'The Christian of today lives in a Diaspora which penetrates deep into the circle of his relatives'—ought not to be overlooked either.

Chapter 2
Before the Council: roots of reform

The cardinals, the princes of the Roman Church, were shocked when the pleasant and rotund old man they had assumed would be a stop-gap pope announced he intended to call an ecumenical council. It was 25 January 1959, and Pope John XXIII (Angelo Roncalli) was speaking to the cardinals at the ancient Roman Basilica of St Paul Outside the Walls, the purported burial site of the greatest Christian evangelist to ever live. Papa Roncalli's aims for the Vatican Council he intended to convene were daring. He explicitly ranked ecumenism—that is, dialogue between separated bodies of Christians with the goal of visible reunion—as a main focus. This was stunning. While there had been some openness to dialogue in certain controlled settings under the previous pope, Pius XII (a cautious revision of earlier, uniformly prohibitive policies), the official Catholic attitude toward Protestants and the Eastern Orthodox was still simple, unambiguous, and triumphalistic: abjure your errors and 'come home to Rome'.

After stating that Catholic doctrine and good church discipline would be reaffirmed, Pope John said Vatican II would give 'a renewed cordial invitation to the faithful of the separated communities [non-Catholic Christians] to participate with us in this quest for unity and grace, for which so many souls long in all parts of the world'. The Council would thus seek 'the enlightenment, edification, and joy of the entire Christian people'. Already, before any formal preparations had begun, the pope was giving the new Council an agenda which combined internal (*ad intra*) renewal with external (*ad extra*) mission to the world. But before embarking on this *Second* Vatican Council, Pope John had to actually formally close the *First* Vatican Council, which had simply been abandoned when Italian troops invaded the Papal States in the summer of 1870. This unceremonious conclusion came just after the bishops at Vatican I voted to proclaim the dogmas of papal infallibility and jurisdictional supremacy—twin prerogatives so sweeping that some wondered if there would ever be another ecumenical council. A certain brand of 'ultramontane' (papal-centric) Catholic wondered how there could be any need for one—couldn't the pope just decide all issues, under the infallible protection of the Holy Spirit? Thus, the act of Pope John calling a council at all—summoning 2,500 of his brother bishops to Rome—was in itself a powerful ecclesiological statement that the Church was not ruled by the pope alone.

There is a story, perhaps apocryphal, that sometime in the 1950s, when Archbishop Angelo Roncalli finished reading the French Dominican priest Yves Congar's controversial book *True and False Reform in the Church*, he asked himself: 'A reform of the church: is such a thing really possible?' On 25 January 1959, less than three months after he was elected Pope John XXIII, Roncalli answered that question himself with a resounding 'yes'. But what did John XXIII, Congar, and others mean by 'reform'? And what were the ways in which they wanted this new ecumenical council to reform the Catholic Church? To better understand these goals and aspirations, we should also examine the deeper roots of Vatican II, which take us back much further than Paris and Rome in the 1950s—to Oxford University in the 1840s, Germany in the aftermath of Napoleon's fall, and Tuscany during the Enlightenment.

Reform and three ways to understand it

At the broadest level, reform is just 'change for the better' (*mutatio in melius*, as the Latin phrase goes). Reform is not a totally new beginning. To merge ecclesial and political metaphors, it is not a revolution, in which some ecclesiastical forces eliminate the existing Church and substitute a new one of their own creation. Reform re-moulds (literally, re-forms) or improves something that already exists, without discarding it. Nevertheless, the word *radical*, with its etymology from *radix* (root, source, origin), is very much applicable to Vatican II. For many of the most significant changes that occurred at and after the Council were intended as a *return* to forgotten or obscured Christian and Catholic roots.

Defining reform as 'change for the better' is too broad to get us very far. It also begs questions involving debatable value judgements. Three concepts, in use before and at the Council, provide us with a stronger conceptual framework for understanding Vatican II's overall project: *aggiornamento*, *ressourcement*, and the development of doctrine. Let us briefly define each of these kinds of reform, while keeping in mind that their boundaries are fluid and they often overlap with each other.

First, the Italian word *aggiornamento*, which we could rather woodenly translate into English as 'updating'. This is a theme that John XXIII made his own through repeated usage, for example when he famously called for the Church to let in 'fresh air'. This 'updating' was not just making disciplinary or administrative changes for pastoral or practical reasons, although it could include those things. Virtually all agree, whether they bemoan it or celebrate it, that a deeper *aggiornamento* occurred at the Council as, indeed, was intended by Pope John: the Catholic Church made peace, or at least attempted to make peace, with certain elements of modernity. This re-presentation of church doctrine involved an updating of political, cultural, and theological ideas. As the historian John O'Malley has driven home, it also involved a thoroughgoing overhaul of rhetoric. Vatican II's documents are quite different from any other ecumenical council in their *tone* and *style* (and indeed length). This is perhaps the chief legacy and import of John XXIII's call for *aggiornamento*. While it can, and often does, rely on traditional ideas, *aggiornamento* has a progressive dynamic. It implies that Catholics must adapt to and even learn from new ideas and attitudes, including those from outside the Church. Consequently, the Church must *listen* and *learn* as well as know and teach.

Second is the French neologism *ressourcement*, coined by the Catholic poet Charles Péguy (killed in the First World War) and popularized in the decades preceding the Council. *Ressourcement* describes an aspect of reform that involves a searching of historical texts and data in order to reapply the theological wisdom of the past to the present. The 'sources' that 20th-century Catholics wanted to return to were the Bible (first and foremost), but also the writings of the great early Christian thinkers (the 'Church Fathers' or 'patristic sources'), and the sources of 'liturgical' life (i.e. public worship, chiefly the Mass). *Ressourcement* also included fresh attention to much later authors like the medieval genius Thomas Aquinas (1225–74), though *ressourcement* theologians insisted on reading him directly, unfiltered through later textbooks and manuals that they found at best boring and at worst distortive. By the 1960s, many theologians like Congar and the German priest (and future pope) Joseph Ratzinger saw *ressourcement* not as one tool in the toolbox but as a general principle, as a new way of doing theology and pastoral practice. *Ressourcement* can challenge the status quo and call for something to replace it. However, it is a fundamentally conservative type of reform insofar as *ressourcement* calls for returning to the past, to the foundations of the faith—scripture, the Fathers, the liturgy—as the sources for desired reforms.

Ressourcement can be inspired by contemporary questions, but it looks to the treasure trove of the past to answer these questions.

Third, reform occurred at Vatican II in the form of the development of doctrine. While the notion of doctrine developing or changing was mostly foreign to early modern Catholicism, due to works like John Henry Newman's *Essay on the Development of Christian Doctrine* (1845), the idea of 'doctrinal development' had become the established way of explaining the coherence (or even the existence) of doctrines that are not explicit in scripture or the earliest Christian sources (such as papal infallibility or Mary's Assumption into heaven). The notion of development is itself embedded in the Vatican II document *Dei Verbum* (see Chapter 5).

Of course, this triadic grid of *aggiornamento*, *ressourcement*, and the development of doctrine is ultimately just a hermeneutical aid to understanding an event of gigantic theological and historical importance. It by no means exhausts everything that can be said about Vatican II, much less about Catholicism and reform. Nevertheless, when we try to tell the story of the lead-up to Vatican II, and when we talk about 'forerunners' of the Council, we mean both that there were Catholics who engaged in *ressourcement* and *aggiornamento* and that some Catholics called for specific reforms that anticipated or even directly influenced the Council's decisions.

Forerunners of Vatican II: from Catholic Enlightenment to *nouvelle théologie*

It is widely acknowledged that Vatican II was the product of a variety of 20th-century figures and movements who engaged in *aggiornamento* and *ressourcement* in their theological writings and pastoral practices. The most common way of telling this story highlights liturgical, patristic, ecumenical, and biblical movements, as well as currents 'from above' (popes and bishops) and 'from below' (priests, religious, associations of laypeople, etc.). We will briefly lay out this common and helpful narrative, but also supplement it with a deeper story that is not as well known, pushing back beyond the 1800s and into the Age of Enlightenment.

Although some Vatican II reforms—like the wide expansion of the use of vernacular languages at Mass (see Chapter 4)—were a real surprise to many, there had long been a liturgical movement in the Church interested in bridging the (perceived) gap between priest and people. This movement is especially associated with Benedictine monks like Lambert Beauduin (1873–1960) and Dom Prosper Guéranger (1805–75), and the communities of Solesmes in France and Collegeville in Minnesota. Liturgical reform was sometimes supported directly 'from above' through a variety of decisions and policies of popes like Pius X (pope from 1903 to 1914) and Pius XII (1939–58). Pius X encouraged frequent reception of the Eucharist and lowered the age of first communion. Though Pius XII was sceptical of the 'new theology', he pushed forward a number of *ressourcement*-inspired liturgical changes including the Holy Week reforms. These new ways of celebrating Holy Thursday, Good Friday, and Easter Saturday and Sunday, which are now cherished by many Catholics, were in fact inspired by more ancient forms of worship.

A biblical movement was championed by figures like Marie-Joseph Lagrange (1855–1938) and the Dominicans of the *École biblique* in Jerusalem. Support 'from above' came with the famous papal encyclicals (teaching letters) *Providentissimus Deus* (1893) of Leo XIII and *Divino afflante Spiritu* (1943) of Pius XII. But the story of papal involvement in 20th-century Catholic reform was by no means a linear one. For example, the biblical movement was stalled by Pius X's ferocious backlash against Catholic (theological) Modernism in the early 1900s. Even moderate claims of historical criticism, such as pointing out that Moses did not write the Pentateuch, could make one suspect in the anti-Modernist climate fostered by Pius X and his advisers.

Liturgy and a prioritization of scripture go together, as emphasized in the Christocentric spiritual renewal embodied by forerunners of Vatican II like Romano Guardini (1885–1968). Many of the figures that played central roles at the Council as *periti* (theological experts who assisted bishops) were at the cutting edge of Catholic reform in the 1940s and 1950s as the vanguards of the controversial *nouvelle théologie* network. The term itself, literally 'new theology', was originally coined by opponents for whom 'novelty' was not counted as a theological virtue. But the name stuck, as such derogatory labels often do, and was eventually proudly embraced by many.

Leaders of the *nouvelle théologie* include innovative French theologians, especially Dominicans like Congar and Marie-Dominique Chenu and Jesuits such as Henri de Lubac and Jean Daniélou. In the decades immediately preceding the Council, *la nouvelle théologie* was the most significant and impactful network among a panoply of diffuse ecclesial phenomena interested in the retrieval of past modes and motifs of Christian thought and action in order to reform stagnant church practices and structures. A few Catholics are still suspicious of the *nouvelle théologie* today, but most (following the Council and the postconciliar popes) celebrate its achievements and insights as prophetic. What is undeniable is that the *nouvelle théologie* went from suspect in the eyes of Rome and many traditional theologians to forming the ecclesial mainstream, so complete was its proponents' rehabilitation and even triumph at Vatican II.

Many genealogies of the Council include idiosyncratic intellectuals like Pierre Teilhard de Chardin (1881–1955) and Modernists such as George Tyrell (1861–1909) and Baron Friedrich von Hügel (1852–1925), but the exact relation between the thought of these figures and Vatican II remains contested. Early 20th-century Catholic Modernism is seen by some as a phantom heresy, by others as a real but exaggerated problem, and by Catholic traditionalists as an uncontained theological virus. Certain parallels (at least) between the questions raised by Modernists and later *ressourcement* figures are undeniable, centred as they were around what Ratzinger, soon after his election as Benedict XVI, called 'a single problem' facing the Catholic Church at Vatican II—the problem of modernity. Modernism was one of the most important 'ghosts' in the Aula (the council hall), influencing how the bishops phrased their ideas or attacked the views of others. By a 'ghost' we mean a key event, text, or movement in the Catholic Church's collective memory which influenced the discussion at Vatican II and the drafting of council documents and subsequent debate over them.

Sometimes the story of the roots of Vatican II is pushed back into the 19th century, often to include the English cardinal St John Henry Newman (1801–90) as an important forerunner. While this subtle and original thinker clearly *anticipated* conciliar thought in a number of areas (patristic *ressourcement*, ecclesiological insights, his profound theology of the laity), it's also true that Newman's work itself was a source, via Congar, for one of the most important and innovative teachings of Vatican II—that doctrine develops. Also, the circle of thinkers in the German Tübingen School (founded 1817) have rightly been called forerunners of the Council, especially the brilliant Johann Adam Möhler (1796–1838).

The merits of this well-worn path notwithstanding, the roots of Vatican II should be further complicated. If the essence of Vatican II reform was *ressourcement*, *aggiornamento*, and the development of doctrine, then we should look beyond Newman and the Tübingen School. Recognizing that the roots of 20th-century Catholic reform stretch back beyond the 19th century and into the age of Enlightenment and Revolution helps us to appreciate the ways in which Vatican II reformed the Catholic Church by better understanding the deep, unresolved questions and problems to which the Council reacted.

During the 1700s, the Catholic Church faced a huge complex of new philosophical, political, and cultural ideas. Although the relationship between Catholicism and Enlightenment was once considered almost purely oppositional—and 'much of the blame' (quoting church historian Ulrich Lehner) for this simplistic narrative can be laid at the feet of intransigent Catholics themselves—the existence of a 'Catholic Enlightenment' is now commonplace in scholarly literature. Many 'enlightened' Catholics, to various degrees and in various ways, participated in *ressourcement* and *aggiornamento.*

For example, the leadership of Prospero Lambertini (Pope Benedict XIV, 1740–58) fostered a cautious but real openness to modern scientific methods, leading to the removal of Copernican books from the Index of Forbidden Books in 1757 (thus implicitly rehabilitating Galileo). Benedict XIV also encouraged critical historical scholarship and, even if rather begrudgingly, increased access to the Bible in the vernacular. The culture fostered by Lambertini also encouraged 'positive' theology rooted in biblical and patristic texts and not necessarily in medieval scholastic method. Benedict's pontificate helped foster the more irenic approaches of enlightened Catholic scholars and theologians. Foremost among these enlightened Catholics was Lodovico Muratori (1672–1750), a parish priest in Modena and one of the greatest historians of his age. Muratori's theological and pastoral writing is, in places, a striking anticipation of 20th-century *ressourcement* Catholicism. In the English-speaking world, figures like John Carroll (1736–1815), the first bishop of the United States, argued in favour of vernacular liturgy and religious liberty. Carroll, a fervent supporter of liberal democracy and the US Constitution, went beyond arguments for the pragmatic toleration of 'error'; Carroll argued that human beings had a right to be free from coercion in religious matters. These ideas had significant support among the oppressed Catholic populations in Ireland and Britain, especially the enlightened 'Cisalpine' (i.e. not ultramontane) network centred in England.

Jansenism, an often caricatured and misunderstood phenomenon, is an important ingredient in the story of the deeper roots of 20th-century Catholic reform. Indeed, perhaps the clearest anticipation of Vatican II in the 18th century was a Jansenist synod. In 1786, the (in)famous Bishop Scipione de' Ricci (1741–1810) held a synod in Pistoia (Tuscany) which enacted a sweeping series of reforms that intrigued and shocked Catholic Europe. These 'Pistoians'—Ricci's correspondents and allies in fact spanned much of Europe and into the Middle East—advocated vernacular Bible reading and a vernacular liturgy. They rejected the coercion of the Inquisition. Infallibility was principally a gift to the whole Church, and the pope was seen as a servant of unity, not an absolute monarch. The goal of Ricci and his collaborators was to create a blueprint for the synodal reform of the entire Church, but their aggression and extremism antagonized the pope and many other Catholics. In the judgement of historian S. J. Miller, the reform efforts that culminated in the Synod of Pistoia 'constitute perhaps the nearest to victory that Enlightened Catholicism came'.

Somewhat ironically, the events set in motion by the French Revolution rewrote the map of Europe and the balance of power in the Church, leading to the dominance of counter-Enlightenment, ultramontane Catholicism. Many of the ideas advocated by irenic moderates like Muratori, English-speaking enlighteners like Carroll, and radicals like the Jansenists of Pistoia clearly anticipated Vatican II and the current teaching and practice of the Catholic Church. A great deal of this reformist agenda, however, was put on ice during an era of ultramontane reaction that triumphed at the First Vatican Council in 1870. Modernism was not the oldest ghost that lurked in the Aula of St Peter's. The Council Fathers had to face up to a long-delayed *rapprochement* with modernity, revisit a slew of reform proposals that some Catholics had called for in past centuries (many of whom were condemned), and re-examine the Church's painful history with Orthodox Christians, Protestants, and the Jews.

Chapter 3
The event of the Council: what happened and when?

The procession of 2,500 bishops, abbots, and cardinals into St Peter's on 11 October 1962 was a sight to behold. The massive and ancient basilica, brimming with baroque pomp, was packed to the rafters with theologians, non-Catholic observers, heads of state, and clergy in a rich variety of ecclesiastical dress. Pope John opened the Council that morning in a famous address called *Gaudet Mater Ecclesia* ('Mother Church rejoices'). Papa Roncalli sounded a Congarian note by stating that, while Catholic dogma cannot and must not be altered, the Church should re-investigate and re-present her teaching 'in the way demanded by our times'. The pope was calling, unmistakably, for a combination of *aggiornamento* and *ressourcement.* As if pre-empting criticism or cynicism about this path of renewal, John wagged the papal finger at those 'prophets of doom' who always 'forecast disaster'. Though he recognized such people 'burn with religious fervour', he distanced himself—and, by implication, the Council—from those Catholics who see 'only ruin and calamity in the present conditions of human society'. Foreshadowing the historical consciousness with which many of the leading Council Fathers and their advisers would operate, Pope John blamed the 'prophets of doom' for naively holding on to golden-age myths about the Catholic past and acting 'as if they have nothing to learn from history, which is the teacher of life'.

Lest we get ahead of ourselves, one might ask how they got from Pope John's announcement in 1959 of a *desire* to convene a council to thousands of people from all over the world actually gathering in St Peter's. It would be hard enough to get 2,500 prelates, many of them ageing or elderly, to begin discussion and deliberation by October 1962—and this is not to mention their entourages and the immense resources needed to house, feed, transport, and support them. Even a cursory brainstorming of the logistics brings on a migraine. The bishops complained of being absolutely inundated with papers and texts they were supposed to read upon arrival—70 documents had been prepared by Roman committees hard at work from 1959 to 1962.

To get a sense of the scale of Vatican II: about 700 bishops attended all or part of the First Vatican Council, which ran only from December 1869 to July 1870. This number was more than were ever present at the Council of Trent (1545–63). Vatican II, at all four sessions, had at least three times as many voting bishops as Vatican I had at its height. The diversity of the languages and ethnic and national backgrounds at Vatican II was unprecedented for an ecumenical council. Catholicism claimed adherents from all over the globe by the 19th century, but the episcopal hierarchy was still very Euro-centric. Not all the Latin-rite bishops at Vatican I were Europeans or North Americans, but all of their parents were. At Vatican II, the exciting challenge of running what O'Malley rightly called 'the largest meeting in world history' is a story in its own right. It has been ably told in great detail elsewhere—from the problem of acoustics to wildly different Latin pronunciations (Boston's Archbishop, Richard Cushing, was particularly difficult to understand) to the absolutely vital installation of espresso bars at the back of St Peter's.

Probably the most important logistical calculations for a smoothly running ecumenical council were concrete, manageable agendas for discussion, and a bureaucratic apparatus capable of ensuring productive debate and voting. To greatly oversimplify an extremely complicated picture, the engines for getting off the ground were the 11 'Commissions' and three 'Secretariats' that John XXIII and his closest advisers established. The Commissions were organized around various topics like Liturgy, Mission, Seminaries, and Catholic Schools. In the preparatory years 1959–62, these bodies solicited the opinions and advice of bishops all over the world. They also met to prepare draft documents (*schemata*; sing. *schema*) that were presented to the Council Fathers when they finally gathered in Rome. The Secretariats were the central bureaucratic agencies of the Council. Four 'Presidents' (leading cardinals chosen by the pope) and a Secretary General (the Italian Archbishop Pericle Felici) were responsible for much of the day-to-day functioning of the sessions.

The bureaucratic logistics of Vatican II are important parts of the story. Some of the highest drama and the best gossip of the Council concerned behind-the-scenes manoeuvring and procedure: from interpersonal strife, to last-second attempts to personally sway the pope for or against a document or amendment, to even the secretive burning of ballots in one case! We will confine our discussions of organizational matters to their bearings on key developments on the Council floor.

There was certainly blame to go around for episodes of mismanagement, not to mention the plain old grudges and prejudices that impeded working relationships. But the fact is that the pope, the Roman Curia, the bishops of the world, and countless other hard-working people managed to pull off the production of 16 final texts (the fruit of various degrees of consensus ranging from high to virtually unanimous) covering a vast range of topics. Fortified with a great deal of patience and endurance, the bureaucracy of the Council managed to provide the conditions necessary for the leaders of a global Church to exchange views in a manner that was, on balance, surprisingly frank and productive. It vastly exceeded what almost all of the participants imagined would be possible in the run-up to the Council. Let us now briefly survey each of Vatican II's four sessions.

> I would hazard a guess that the different commissions will get to work rapidly, and from time to time will send statements to the bishops throughout the world for comments, views, etc., so that when the time comes for the meeting of the Council itself, there will not be any occasion for prolonged discussions...
>
> Thus the preparations will proceed pretty rapidly and when the Council comes to be held—perhaps in 1962?—there will be no need for any long sessions: maybe some weeks will be sufficient...
>
> [Scrawled in margin at a later date:] Wrong!
>
> **Matthew Beovich (1896–1981)**, diary entries in July 1960
>
> Archbishop of Adelaide (Australia), 1940–71

The First Session (1962): a 'majority' and a 'minority' come into focus

When the Council Fathers arrived in Rome in the autumn of 1962, some of them, possibly even most of them, believed the Council could conclude its business in one session. A rapid conclusion became impossible for two reasons. First, the sheer magnitude of the task soon became apparent to everybody. Second, it did not take long for a majority bloc to form within the Council that refused to rubber-stamp the documents prepared for them by the preparatory Commissions. This set Vatican II on a new and unpredictable course—one that energized widespread reformist energy from North America to East Asia and captured the attention of non-Catholics and the world press, but also caused serious alarm in quarters interested in preserving the status quo.

Each of the four sessions of the Council from 1962 to 1965 ran for two to three months, from September or early October to late November or early December. No documents were formally approved in the First Session, but some pivotal debates took place which laid the groundwork for the entire written *corpus* that Vatican II eventually produced, and especially for two key 'Constitutions': one on the liturgy and one on divine revelation.

On 14 November, the same day that the Council Fathers voted overwhelmingly in favour of liturgical reform, they turned to the *schema* (draft text) on Divine Revelation called *De Fontibus* (referring to the founts or sources of scripture and tradition). Disagreement over how to present the Catholic understanding of God's self-revelation to humanity set the stage for the next three years by clearly highlighting a reformist 'Majority' bloc and a more cautious 'Minority'. When session one ended in December 1962, the Majority had strongly asserted itself by rejecting the *De Fontibus* text. Behind the seemingly basic and foundational task of drafting a document on Revelation lay a number of contentious, challenging issues: the best theological method and style for the Council to adopt, the relationship between scripture and tradition (and the nature of 'Tradition' itself), the duties (or not) of ecumenism, and the normativity of past practices and doctrinal pronouncements (what we could call their 'controlling function'). Ghosts from the Modernist crisis and the Reformation era haunted the Council Fathers during these debates (see Chapter 5).

Before we move on, let us examine these two opposed tendencies that emerged in the First Session and held up to a significant extent throughout the rest of the Council. The *numerical* descriptors 'Minority' and 'Majority' are meant to militate against overly partisan interpretations of Vatican II (which are, unfortunately, still common), while still explaining the fairly consistent divisions that clearly *were* present over matters of both style and of substance. They are preferable to labels like 'conservative', 'orthodox', 'liberal', or 'progressive'—these depend too much on one's ideological context and often conceal veiled value judgements, though such tags can still be useful at times.

It was as motley a group of 'non-Catholics' as ever had been assembled. We were often referred to as 'the observers corps'—an obvious misnomer. Actually, we were a mélange, not only with widely different backgrounds but with differing concerns and differing degrees of wariness. We were not organized and our traditions had had widely different dealings with Rome... Moreover, our expectations of the Council differed almost categorically. There were [some who] feared another Roman 'trap'. More numerous were the 'skeptics', who simply doubted the Council's intention to crack the *status quo* by much. Still more numerous were the 'realists' whose highest hopes envisaged a somewhat more cordial co-existence with Rome, without much change on either side. Finally, there were the 'visionaries', who had come to see the Council itself as a sort of miracle in its own right, and who found it, therefore, credible to hope for something more. We were a distinct minority.

Albert Outler (1908–89), writing in 1984

American Methodist theologian and philosopher; official ecumenical 'observer' at Vatican II

The labels Majority and Minority are also preferred since they refer to something objectively quantifiable—that is, how Council Fathers actually voted on proposed texts. Majority members like Cardinals Josef Frings (Cologne) and Franz König (Vienna), and their *periti*, the German theologians Joseph Ratzinger (Figure 2) and Karl Rahner SJ, generally identified with John XXIII's *aggiornamento* and with *ressourcement* theology. The Minority, which probably never made up more than 15–20 per cent of the total voting members, typically opposed deviations from the status quo not only in substance but also in style. Its de facto leader, Cardinal Ottaviani, head of the Holy Office (i.e., the Vatican department charged with policing doctrine), accordingly became something of

2. Council *periti* (i.e. 'experts') Joseph Ratzinger and Yves Congar OP.

a *bête noire* to the Council Majority. In one case, vigorous applause congratulated a moderator for enforcing a time limit, cutting off a combative speech by Ottaviani that was running long. The world press tended to vilify him as an intransigent. Ottaviani would not entirely disown such a characterization. His episcopal motto, after all, was *Semper Idem*: 'always the same'.

Of course, as with any binary, we are dealing with very broad and at times fluid realities. For example, depending on the issue, someone might look startlingly 'progressive' to modern Western eyes and then shockingly 'conservative' or traditionalist on another topic. For example, as we will see, Cardinal Ottaviani staunchly opposed liturgical change and any deviation from what he saw as traditional doctrine (up to and including on religious liberty), and yet he spoke out forcefully regarding the incompatibility of Catholic moral teaching with modern means of warfare, especially the nuclear bomb. Many American bishops, especially, had precisely the opposite convictions.

This first great debate that broke out in November 1962 provided a rough road map for the direction of the Council and exposed these key divisions. In contrast to the *relatively* pacific deliberations over liturgical reform, tension escalated quickly when *De Fontibus* came to the floor for discussion. According to the Council's official regulations, a two-thirds majority was required to reject a draft text. On 20 November, 1,368 Council Fathers voted to send *De Fontibus* back for re-drafting (a de facto rejection of the text), while 822 voted to keep it. A clear majority had voted to reject, but it was about 100 votes short of the required two-thirds. John XXIII decided that it was not in the Council's best interests to continue debate on a document so many Fathers were unhappy with, even though the number technically fell short of the formal regulations. The pope also—and this was critical—appointed a new 'Mixed Commission' to oversee the re-drafting. This new Commission would combine members of Ottaviani's Theological Commission with the Secretariat for Christianity Unity, led by the Cardinal Augustin Bea, a German Jesuit and an important Majority leader. Pope John's decision, then, was both a nod to the numerical significance of the Majority and a reminder of his own commitment to producing ecumenical texts.

When the First Session closed on 8 December 1962, the Council Fathers knew that the task before them was a momentous one. They had completed no documents, but they had held productive discussions regarding the reform of the liturgy and the Majority effectively asserted itself against the status quo. When they departed Rome to return to their home dioceses for Christmas, the Council Fathers did not know that a new pope would sit on the Chair of St Peter when they reconvened.

Session two (1963): the great debate on the Church begins

John XXIII's death on 3 June 1963 caused an eruption of grief and sympathy around the world. Weeks before he died, John published the encyclical *Pacem in Terris* ('Peace on Earth'). This new contribution to Catholic social teaching unambiguously taught that religious liberty was a positive good and a right, and the pope addressed it to 'all people of good will'. Leaders of the Majority pushing for an *ad extra* posture of dialogue, like Cardinal Suenens, now had an increasingly codified papal mandate favouring this approach.

The death of a pope causes an ecumenical council to be automatically suspended. There was never really a doubt that the next pope would reconvene the Council, but the manner in which he would guide or direct it was the central issue in the election. When white smoke plumed out of the Sistine Chapel on 21 June, the Archbishop of Milan, Cardinal Giovanni Montini, emerged as Pope Paul VI. Montini was a complex and cautious man, kind and thoughtful but not ebullient like John XXIII. With the Majority, he took a generally positive approach to calls for *aggiornamento* and *ressourcement*, and he agreed that the *De Fontibus* draft was insufficient. In his speech opening the Second Session on 29 September, Pope Paul reiterated John XXIII's goals and added his support to the Majority's desire to examine the office of bishop and its relationship to the papacy.

The Second Session was marked by an important bureaucratic streamlining that improved the logistics of the Council. The mass of texts was cut down to a manageable, though still imposing, 17 (16 would eventually be 'promulgated', which is the technical term used for when the pope formally approves and issues a church document). The bulk of the session in October and November was marked by contentious and protracted debate on 'ecclesiology'—that is, the nature of the Catholic Church itself (see Chapter 6). The same fault-lines exposed by *De Fontibus* were glaring when Cardinal Ottaviani introduced the schema *De Ecclesia* ('On the Church') at the end of session one.

De Ecclesia, now called *Lumen Gentium* ('Light of the Nations'), was ambitious in scope. It concerned not only fundamental theological doctrines, but also matters that promised to impact the practical, day-to-day functioning of the worldwide Catholic Church. This combination of factors led to the most explosive debates of the Council. These debates, which ran through the next session, were wide ranging: the role of the laity, the nature of the Church as 'sacrament', teaching on the Virgin Mary, ecumenism, and the Church's relationship with the Jewish people all saw discussion. In the shadows lurked the future of the millennium-and-older discipline of clerical celibacy for Latin-rite Catholic clergy, though the pope ultimately banned discussion of the issue. But the question that strained the unity of the bishops to a degree not seen since papal infallibility was debated 100 years prior at Vatican I was the related doctrine of 'episcopal collegiality'—that is, the co-responsibility for governing the Church that all bishops shared. In the teeth of significant and well-organized opposition, the Majority won a resounding victory in an episode on 30 October, when five questions put to the assembly for a vote revealed very strong support for episcopal collegiality. When the Second Session drew to a close, the question was *how* the Council would reform and re-present ecclesiological teaching and practice, not whether it would.

On 4 December, the final day of the session, Paul VI presided over the assembly, and the first two texts were officially promulgated—*Sacrosanctum Concilium* (Constitution on the Liturgy) and *Inter Mirifica* (Decree on the Media of Social Communication). Despite the challenges and even turmoil at times, the Council was beginning to see concrete results.

Session three (1964): ghosts on the Council floor

Despite the stormy debates of the Second Session, the third opened on 14 September 1964 with a sense of optimism for those favouring a reformist approach. Paul VI's pilgrimage to the Holy Land included sincere overtures to Jews and the Eastern Orthodox (see Chapter 7). Both the pilgrimage and the nature of the pope's conversations and addresses were unprecedented in the last 500 years and led to an equally warm reception from the Orthodox Patriarch Athenagoras. This seemed like a confirmation of the dialogical and ecumenical turn the Council had taken. Cardinal Suenens's rather unarguable contention at the end of the Second Session that since women make up half the human race ('if I'm not mistaken', he wryly added) and therefore should be represented at the Council led to the small but symbolically momentous addition of 23 women (10 of them women religious) to the Council as 'auditors'. Though these may seem like paltry figures—as indeed they are—this was, by ecclesiastical standards, a bold new departure. This incident was both an expansion and a realization of Vatican II's emphasis on a baptismal ecclesiology, in which the entire People of God were co-workers in the Body of Christ with their priests and bishops. The debates in the Aula were already changing Catholicism, and the documents on ecumenism and on the Church were not even published yet.

Intense ecclesiological struggle continued without much respite. Controversies over draft texts on religious liberty and on the Church in the modern world (which became *Dignitatis Humanae* and *Gaudium et Spes*) flared up and were not resolved until the next and final session. However, tangible achievement came on 21 November 1964, when three interrelated ecclesiological texts were promulgated: *Lumen Gentium* (Dogmatic Constitution on the Church), *Unitatis Redintegratio* (Decree on Ecumenism), and *Orientalium*

> That women auditors were at the Council...was at least an important first step...
>
> For me, in regard to the status of women, Vatican II was an opening, although just a tiny crack in the door, to a recognition of the vast indifference to women and the ignoring of their potential for the whole body of the church.
>
> **Mary Luke Tobin SL (1908–2006)**, writing in 1985
>
> Superior-General of the Sisters of Loretto, 1958–70, and President, Leadership Congregation of Women Religious (USA), 1964–6; official 'auditor' during Third and Fourth Sessions

Ecclesiarum ('Decree on the Catholic Churches of the Eastern Rite'; i.e. non-Roman Catholics). The texts of these documents, often serene, inspiring, and far-reaching, mask the great pains that brought them forth.

In the final week of the Third Session, these ecclesiological tensions all came to a head. The so-called 'Black Week' of 16–20 November saw some of the most dramatic episodes of the Council. Paul VI intervened decisively to amend the ecumenism decree, postpone the vote on the religious liberty text, and add an interpretative appendix to *Lumen Gentium*, which concerned episcopal collegiality and other fraught questions of the relationship between the pope and the bishops. In order to calm the fears of the Minority, and to avoid readings of collegiality that he believed were ambiguous or wrong, Paul VI decreed that a *Nota explicativa praevia* (explanatory note) be appended to *Lumen Gentium*. The Council Fathers of the Majority were disturbed by this act of papal fiat, especially coming at the eleventh hour. They were being asked to sign material that the conciliar commissions had not drafted and the Council Fathers had not been able to discern, debate, or vote on. And, with grim irony, this material concerned the relationship between papal and episcopal authority. It was the very issue they had struggled for so long to assert some independence over.

The *Nota*, drafted in large part by the Louvain theologian Gérard Philips—himself a chief architect of the main text of *Lumen Gentium*—bent over backwards to make clear that whatever episcopal collegiality meant, it could in no way impede or detract from papal supremacy and the prerogatives outlined at Vatican I. Members of the Minority had impressed upon Pope Paul VI the possibility of problematic interpretations of the doctrine of collegiality as the text of *Lumen Gentium* stood. They raised, in the words of Yves Congar, the 'spectre of Pistoia'—the memory of the Jansenist synod of 1786, solemnly condemned by Pope Pius VI, that sought to restrict papal power by insisting that the authority of diocesan bishops, coming from God, was inviolable (see Chapter 2). Staunch opponents of collegiality like the Italian bishop Luigi Carli had several times evoked this 'ghost' of Pistoia but could not convince the Majority. Paul VI, ultimately, did not need to convince anyone—he appended this 'explanatory note' on his own authority.

Despite these tensions, session three had brought some big ships to port in this trifecta of ecclesiological documents. The Minority could take comfort in the fact that this unpredictable ecumenical council had not spiralled out of control into a repudiation of papal supremacy or a democratization of the Church. The Majority, who wanted reform and not revolution, knew that they had at least begun the process of 'balancing' Vatican I's lopsided ultramontanism. Whatever the ecclesiological texts of Vatican II did or did not say, they were certainly not simply restatements of Vatican I or the neo-scholastic textbooks of the 1950s. Catholicism, consequently, would never be the same.

Session four (1965): a Church in and for the world

The last session of Vatican II was something like the exciting, frantic, and stressful final days of a school term, in which there is a rush to turn in all the work before the end of the semester. A bewildering 11 documents were promulgated in late 1965—recall only five were over the previous three sessions. This brought the total output of the Council to 16 texts—four 'Constitutions', nine 'Decrees', and three 'Declarations'. The sheer size of the Vatican II *corpus* is staggering for an ecumenical council, dwarfing the word count length of the entire Council of Trent, which was by no means a hasty affair.

Discussions in session four continued many of the ecclesiological themes of the previous years, but with a much stronger focus on the Church *in* the world, and the manner in which the Church should relate *to* the world. Paul VI's actions mirrored these concerns. In December 1964, he travelled to India for a eucharistic congress. A Roman pope visiting a vast non-Western nation was yet another precedent breaker, and particularly poignant given the issues the Council was set to debate. India, home to an ancient civilization, was marked by extreme poverty, recent decolonization, and thriving non-Western religions—issues near and dear to the major texts of the Fourth Session: the Pastoral Constitution on the Church in the Modern World, called *Gaudium et Spes*, and the Declaration on Non-Christian Religions, *Nostra Aetate.*

Three weeks after the Fourth Session opened on 14 September 1965, Paul VI addressed the United Nations in New York and celebrated Mass in Yankee Stadium. These kinds of 'world stage' actions cast Catholicism as a Church not only with diverse membership but with a global vision. It also anticipated the globetrotting 'celebrity' papacy of John Paul II, and the (connected) contemporary notion of the pope as a kind of *world* religious and ethical leader, not just the head of the Catholic Church. The discussions in the Aula reflected this vastly expanded focus. Though Europeans still led the debates in many ways, to say that Catholicism could no longer be reduced to a religion of Europeans would be a profound understatement.

The Council Fathers, especially in their discussions of *Gaudium et Spes*, debated a massive complex of social, political, and economic issues. Though marriage and family life was treated, the particularly neuralgic issue of birth control was relegated to a special papal commission and consequently removed from discussion (officially, anyway—the Belgian Cardinal Suenens had already caused a commotion by suggesting continued bans would be seen as a 'second Galileo case').

The advocates of religious liberty, led by the American Jesuit John Courtney Murray and the Italian *peritus* Pietro Pavan (one of the drafters of John XXIII's *Pacem in Terris*), navigated a number of landmines to successfully convince most of the Council Fathers that a stunning change in official church teaching could be justified through the principles of *aggiornamento* and *ressourcement*. The debate over religious liberty clearly shows that the development of doctrine—which everyone could *in theory* accept in some form—was a principal 'issue under the issues' at Vatican II. Almost three out of 10 Council Fathers had opposed the Declaration on Religious Liberty at some stage, or had reservations about it.

The 11 documents of the Fourth Session were promulgated in three big batches. On 28 October the Council Fathers formally approved, and the pope signed, *Gravissimum Educationis* (on Christian education), *Optatam Totius* (on priestly formation), *Christus Dominus* (on the role of bishops), *Perfectae Caritatis* (on the renewal of religious life), and *Nostra Aetate* (on non-Christian religions). Three weeks later, on 18 November, *Apostolicam Actuositatem* (on the laity) was approved. And, bringing everything full circle, the Constitution on Divine Revelation was promulgated as *Dei Verbum*. Then, on 7 December the work of the Council concluded with *Gaudium et Spes*, *Dignitatis Humanae* (on religious liberty), *Ad Gentes* (on missionary activity), and *Presbyterorum Ordinis* (on the priesthood).

That same day, Pope Paul VI and Athenagoras, the (Eastern Orthodox) ecumenical patriarch of Constantinople, mutually lifted their predecessors' infamous excommunications of each other in 1054. Coupled with the profound shifts in official rhetoric and attitudes towards the Jewish people, this event illustrated Vatican II's deep commitment to ecumenical and interreligious healing. The next day, the Council was solemnly concluded when Paul VI celebrated Mass on the Feast of Mary's Immaculate Conception (8 December) in the presence of all the Council Fathers and a crowd of 300,000 people spilling out of St Peter's piazza. The most important religious event of the 20th century was over. Probably no one felt more thankful to God as they intoned *Deo gratias* at the end of Mass than the thousands of Council participants who could finally return home.

Chapter 4
Liturgy

The convention of naming church documents by their opening words (the 'incipit'), combined with the flexibility of Latin word order, means that it's relatively easy for them to be assigned a fittingly symbolic title. Hence *Lumen Gentium* ('Light of the nations') on the Church, *Dei Verbum* ('The word of God') on revelation, and *Inter Mirifica* ('Among the wondrous things') on media technologies. Vatican II's Constitution on the Sacred Liturgy might seem, therefore, to be a strange exception: *Sacrosanctum Concilium* ('[This] Sacred Council') does not obviously brand it as being focused on worship or ritual.

This was, however, no oversight. As the first document to be promulgated—on 4 December 1963, at the tail-end of the Second Session—it was a natural opportunity for the Council to 'set out its store', and indeed to reiterate to the world that the late John XXIII's vision was being continued by Paul VI. The chosen title also emphasized the centrality of the liturgy to the life of the Church (a key theme of the text as a whole), and thus of reforming the former to the renewal of the latter. Accordingly, the text opens with a succinct, four-point manifesto for the whole conciliar project: (1) 'to impart an ever increasing vigour to the Christian life of the faithful'; (2) 'to adapt more suitably to the needs of our own times those institutions which are subject to change'; (3) 'to foster whatever can promote union among all who believe in

It is necessary to adapt the liturgy, and to free it from the heavy armour which for four hundred years has been paralyzing it... This Council will 'thaw out' that which has been frozen in the liturgy, but we must proceed with prudence and caution lest we provoke an inundation.

Henri Jenny (1904–82), press conference in October 1962

Auxiliary bishop of Cambrai (France) and member of Liturgy Commission; appointed Archbishop of Cambrai following Council

Christ'; and (4) 'to strengthen whatever can help to call the whole of mankind into the household of the Church'.

Points 1 and 4 are clearly pastoral and evangelistic in intent, and presuppose the recognition that the Church had, until then, not been doing as well as it might have in these areas. Point 3 is straightforwardly ecumenical. And point 2, essentially concerned with *aggiornamento*, is perhaps best seen as helping the Church to accomplish the other three. These are, then, the Council's own goals for ecclesial self-improvement. And it is therefore *these* which, it goes on to state, constitute 'particularly cogent reasons for undertaking the reform and promotion of the liturgy' (SC 1). They also, of course, set out a clear set of Key Performance Indicators, by which the success or failure of the *actual* reforms might—at least in theory—be judged.

Liturgy at the Council

The liturgy was at the very heart of the life of the Council. Major events—openings and closings of sessions, major feast days, important anniversaries—were marked with special Masses, often lasting several hours (bearing in mind that a solemn procession of 2,000-or-so bishops, abbots, and assorted other prelates into and out of a church takes a fair bit of time in itself). A typical day 'in session' began, moreover, with a Mass, celebrated by one or—especially later on, once *Sacrosanctum Concilium* had enshrined 'concelebration' as the order of the day—more of the Council Fathers. These spanned the full range of Catholic rites, from both West (e.g. the then-Archbishop of Milan, Cardinal Montini, celebrated in the Ambrosian Rite during the First Session) and East, including the ancient Alexandrian Coptic (Egypt) and Ge'ez (Ethiopia) rites, the Syro-Malabar *Qurbana* (India), and the various Byzantine/Greek divine liturgies of *inter alia* the Ukrainian, Slovak, and Melkite particular Churches. These liturgies were especially significant, given the sheer diversity of languages, rubrics, and musics they comprised, and the lack of exposure most Latin-riters would have had to any of them, outside of specific diaspora communities in their home dioceses. The daily diaries of several bishops attest to the striking impression made by these authentically *Catholic* ways of manifesting the joint 'source' and 'summit' of the faith (§§14, 10), however alien they sometimes seemed ('The chanting was strange to my ears,' noted Adelaide's Archbishop Beovich of one Coptic Mass).

While *Sacrosanctum Concilium* confined most of its practical norms to the Latin rite alone, its overarching principles 'can and should be applied... also to all the other rites' (§3). Given this wide-ranging scope, on top of focusing on so central an aspect of church life, it is all the more noteworthy how problem free the document's passage through the Council was. That is to say, the substance of the original liturgy schema, as drawn up by the Preparatory Commission, remains recognizable in the final Constitution. This was helped by there being much continuity in personnel between the original drafters and those appointed to the liturgy subcommission, responsible for guiding the final text through the conciliar process. This is itself a mark of the Council Fathers' satisfaction with the initial text. It also contrasts strongly with the fate of several of the other preparatory schemata, not least those whose *topics*, if not the texts themselves, would eventually furnish Vatican II's other two Dogmatic Constitutions:

De Fontibus Revelatione ('on the sources of revelation') and *De Ecclesia* ('on the Church').

'Problem free' is, admittedly, a comparative term here. On various points, big and small, the *Schema de sacra liturgia* ('draft-text on the sacred liturgy') generated a good deal of heated debate on the Council floor, which could range 'from a conservative hold-the-line attitude to a far-out appeal for change' in a single morning (as Bishop Forst of Dodge City, Kansas, recounted of 22 October 1962). Language was an obvious point of contention, with forceful views expressed on the overriding primacy of Latin in the liturgy, juxtaposed with equally strong ones stressing the pastoral utility of vernacular languages. So too, at various times, were concelebration, the precise scope of stated plans for 'revising' the Order of Mass (cf. §50), the advisability of making the Mass more palatable to Protestant sensibilities, and the possibilities for significant cultural adaptations in mission lands. Interventions regarding the latter gained particular credibility when voiced by those from the small-but-growing ranks of homegrown Asian and African prelates, who were gradually replacing European missionary bishops. This existing trend towards 'decolonizing' the episcopate—evidenced at the Council most obviously with Cardinals Doi of Tokyo, Santos of Manila, Gracias of Bombay, and Rugambwa of Bakoba (modern-day Tanzania)—would accelerate in the years following (Figure 3).

The cut-and-thrust of debates in the Aula and the press (which antagonists often found a more useful way of disseminating their views) ought not, however, to distract from the fundamental consensus that surrounded the liturgy *schema*. Even the most 'hold-the-line' of bishops recognized the need for changes, albeit prudent and cautious ones. And few of the 'far-out appeal for change' ones were able, at this early stage, to imagine just how swiftly things really could and *would* change in even a few years' time. Profane as it might sound to pious ears, there is a good deal of politicking and gamesmanship that goes on at ecumenical

The real difficulty (I think) is that Continentals are twisting themselves inside out to make us look as like as possible to the Protestants. How I wish we could persuade them (a large majority I fear) that to be at home with our Mass and ceremonies is far more important than being right according to the books of liturgical antiquities.

John Heenan (1905–75), letter to Evelyn Waugh, November 1962

Archbishop of Liverpool (England), 1957–63, and Westminster, 1963–75; appointed cardinal, 1965

3. Bishops at Vatican II.

councils. And there is a genuine sense in which many (though admittedly not all) of the liturgy debates were a kind of 'haggling over the details' in a document the vast majority were basically happy with. Indeed, the final vote on it passed with 2,147 voting *placet* (literally 'it pleases') to just 4 against—an approval rating of 99.8 per cent, the highest of any of the conciliar corpus.

Such liturgical harmony did not last long.

Active participation

Crucial to the liturgical vision of Vatican II is the Latin phrase *participatio actuosa*, normally translated into English as 'active participation' (though note that *actuosus* has a subtly different semantic range from *activus*, which is the more direct Latin equivalent of 'active'; hence some scholars argue for 'engaged' as a better rendering). Neither the term, nor the ways in which it is deployed, are novel to *Sacrosanctum Concilium*. Indeed, the idea, and often the exact phrase, had been a staple of magisterial pronouncements on the liturgy for a good 60 years: these included Pius X's *Tra le Sollicetudini* (1903), Pius XI's *Divini Cultus* (1928), and Pius XII's *Mediator Dei* (1947). The basic theme could also be found in spiritual and devotional writing over this period. Thus Reginald Garrigou-Lagrange OP, writing in 1938: 'The sanctification of our soul is found in a daily increasing intimate union with God... Hence the most exalted act of religion and of Christian worship, namely, the participation in the sacrifice of the Mass, is one of the greatest means of sanctification.'

As this quotation makes clear, the primary object of such *participatio, actuosa* or otherwise, is not so much the liturgy as an end in itself, but the life of God. This is why, for example, the Council speaks of the 'earthly liturgy' as 'a foretaste of that heavenly liturgy... where Christ is sitting at the right hand of God' (§8), and why it foregrounds the idea of the paschal mystery as being 'the work of salvation... around which the entire liturgical life revolves' (§6). Participation in the Church's liturgical and sacramental life—and above all in the Mass—is thus the pre-eminent means *through* which Christians are 'given access to the stream of divine grace which flows from the paschal mystery of the passion, death, the resurrection of Christ' (§61).

In large measure, the entire document is oriented around the idea that, since 'fully conscious and active participation... is demanded by the very nature of the liturgy', then this 'full and active participation by all the people is the aim to be considered before all else' (§14). Accordingly, it is the clergy's sacred duty to 'ensure that the faithful take part fully aware of what they are doing, actively engaged in the rite, and enriched by its effects' (§11). This participation is, of course, at root an interior one, as per the gospel injunction to 'love the Lord your God with all your heart, and with all your soul, and with all your mind' (Matthew 22:34). As the French *peritus* Louis Bouyer, who worked on the document, wrote in 1964: 'It is not by making people constantly stand up, sit down or kneel down, while shouting incessantly as soon as they are not talked to, that we shall make them participate. Public and collective prayer does not mean an exclusion of private and personal prayer. Far from it, it is intended to foster it.'

To help do exactly that, several ways of involving the laity more in liturgical celebrations had been tried in the decades preceding the Council. The best known of these was the so-called 'dialogue Mass', in which some of the (Latin) responses, hitherto uttered by altar servers 'on behalf of' the people, were given back to the congregation to say or sing. Some variants also encouraged them to join in with certain prayers. Such Masses were relatively popular in continental Europe, especially in religious houses and at places keen to engage the youth, such as university chaplaincies, though less so elsewhere. They were also, underlining how mainstream the idea was by then, the default way in which morning Masses were celebrated at the Council.

Prior to the Council, provision of—and indeed permission for—these and other experiments in promoting 'active participation in the liturgy both internally and externally' (§19) was patchy and uneven. The Council was thus keen to put its weight behind such efforts: 'To promote active participation, the people should be encouraged to take part by means of acclamations, responses, psalmody, antiphons, and songs, as well as by actions, gestures, and bodily attitudes' (§30).

The vernacular

Of all the changes wrought by Vatican II, the rapid and widespread vernacularization—and attendant de-Latinization—of the liturgy was the most visible, and the one with most direct impact on the laity. One Sunday, Mass was all in Latin (with a small amount of Greek). This was, so far as most people were concerned, as it essentially always had been. The next Sunday, significant bits were suddenly in Spanish, Igbo, Arabic, or Konkani. Thereafter, *which* bits might differ from week to week, or from place to place, but trending overwhelmingly towards a de facto eclipse of Latin in the liturgy (with at most a vestigial *Agnus Dei*, *Gloria*, and/or *Sanctus*) in most parishes. The exact timings varied depending on diocese, country (the initial 'Vernacular Sunday' was on 29 November 1964 in Britain and America, but on 7 March 1965 in Ireland, for example), and language. But the basic pattern was similar in most places.

To the casual, or perhaps naive, reader of *Sacrosanctum Concilium*, this overall result might have come as some surprise. The text itself would seem to be quite plain on this score: 'the use of the Latin language is to be preserved in the Latin rites' (§36, 1). However, the pastoral utility of vernacular languages (i.e. the actual languages spoken and understood by the people) was something that was urged by a large number of the bishops, both in their preconciliar suggestions (*vota*), and on the Council floor. Furthermore, a good number of them were conscious of their own struggles with Latin; asked about what he had said in one of his own interventions, Boston's Cardinal Cushing quipped, 'How should I know, I had to say it in Latin!' Perhaps sitting through hour after hour of poorly amplified, heavily accented speeches in St Peter's Basilica made them reflect on their own ability to participate 'fully aware of what they are doing, actively engaged in' (§11) the debates.

Obviously, one could—and several Fathers did—make the *ressourcement*-ish point that liturgies in the earliest Christian communities, beginning with the Last Supper, were in the ordinary languages of those present. Furthermore, the original Western shift to Latin from Greek and/or Aramaic had itself been to 'ensure that the faithful take part fully aware of what they are doing' (§11). Although equally, one might also argue that, if doctrinal development is a good and necessary thing, then why not also liturgical development? On this view, weight should be given to the organic *maturing* of the liturgy over the centuries—that is, earlier isn't necessarily better—and indeed to the fact that the Western Church had stuck with Latin long after it had stopped being the common tongue. As we shall see in Chapter 7, the mid-20th century presented Vatican II with plenty of new 'matters arising' to comprehend and respond to. But a distance between the liturgical language and what most people could readily understand was, by then, well over a millennium old.

Christ spoke the language of his contemporaries. It was also in the language understood by his hearers, Aramaic, that he offered the first eucharistic Sacrifice. The apostles and disciples did the same. It would never have occurred to them that in a Christian assembly the celebrant could read scriptural passages or sing psalms or preach or 'break bread' using a language other than that of the assembly…

The Latin language is dead. But the Church is alive; and language, the vehicle of grace and of the Holy Spirit, must also be alive, for it is for men and not for angels. No language must be untouchable.

Maximos IV Saigh (1878–1967), Council speech, 23 October 1962

Patriarch of Antioch, and head of Melkite Greek Catholic Church, since 1948

Judicious use of the vernacular was not without more recent precedent, however. Piecemeal, ad hoc permissions had already been granted over the course of the preceding decades. While some Fathers certainly did envisage a near wholesale vernacularization of the Mass, many 'pro-vernacularists' simply wanted a more widespread roll-out of existing options. As the Dutch liturgy commission member Wilhelm van Bekkum, who was Bishop of Ruteng in Indonesia, put it in an October 1962 interview: 'If we consider the dispensations and privileges granted to this or that diocese, to this or that country, we must say that if these privileges become common practice throughout the Church, especially in the mission countries, few of our problems will remain unsolved.' It also did not go unnoticed that the vernacular was perfectly normal in some of the Eastern Catholic Churches. Melkite liturgies had been in Arabic—the ordinary language of Syrian Christians—since the 17th century. Priests ministering to the Melkite diaspora in America, moreover, had been using English for some years (much to the consternation of local Latin-rite bishops).

Immediately following its insistence on the preservation of Latin, therefore, *Sacrosanctum Concilium* offers one of its characteristic 'But...' segues. Recognizing that 'the use of the mother tongue... frequently may be of great advantage to the people', the text decrees: 'the limits of its employment may be extended. This will apply in the first place to the readings and directives, and to some of the prayers and chants...' (§36, 2). Whether, to what extent, and in what translations these permissions are to be applied (as indeed what they might amount to 'in the second place') are then left to the discretion of the local bishops. In practice, this would be the national bishops' conferences—or in some cases regional/linguistic confederations of these, as already being pioneered in Latin America and southern Africa—which were being promoted elsewhere at the Council. While such decisions would still require the 'approval' of the Holy See, such devolution in itself represents a notable shift in ecclesiology.

This general pattern recurs elsewhere. For example, there are paeans to 'the musical tradition of the universal Church' as 'a treasure of inestimable value' (§112) to 'be preserved and fostered with great care' (§114), as well as to the organ as a 'traditional musical instrument which adds a wonderful splendour to the Church's ceremonies and powerfully lifts up man's mind to God and to higher things' (§120). In both cases there immediately follow 'But...' sentences, which open up the possibility of 'other kinds of sacred music' and 'other instruments', should the relevant bishops judge them suitable. Similarly balanced statements can be seen in the passages on popular devotions, priests praying the Daily Office in Latin, and the tradition of nuptial Masses (§§13, 78, 101).

New order

In a real sense, *Sacrosanctum Concilium* amounts to a remarkable exercise in liturgical deregulation. That is to say, while expressing strong preferences for certain traditional ways of doing things, it opens up no end of *possibilities* for 'adapt[ing] more suitably to the needs of our own times' (§1). *If*, that is, such adaptations genuinely do contribute to 'the sacrifice of the Mass, even in the ritual forms of its celebration, becom[ing] pastorally efficacious to the fullest degree' (§49). In practice, this permits a very high degree of customization, even while staying well within officially permitted bounds. The celebration of Mass in the Latin rite before the Council was not, it is true, absolutely uniform. But it is undoubtedly true that this variation (no music or chant or organ; 'dialogue' or not?) admitted of a very much lower 'standard deviation' than it has since.

Alongside what one might call the Council's *permissions*, however, it also issued a number of far-reaching *prescriptions*. Some of these, as for example with a simplification of some of the rubrics for celebrating Mass, were implemented, in fairly short order, to the *existing* 1962 Missal (i.e. with the first phase of

The Order of the Mass has been such for many centuries; the Mass is the centre of the whole of liturgical worship; a most holy thing, well known to each of the faithful and the danger is not of causing surprise, but rather that of scandal due to excessive change. It is about a most holy thing that cannot freely be changed during one age. It is about a most holy thing that should be treated in a holy and venerable manner, and only with difficulty it ought to be touched . . . We ought to be careful about proposing changes to the Mass.

Alfredo Ottaviani (1890–1979), Council speech, 30 October 1962

Italian cardinal since 1953, and Secretary of the Holy Office, 1959–66

vernacularization in Advent 1964). A more thorough attempt came soon after, with the 1965 *Ordo Missae* ('Order of Mass') in the spring of that year. To the casual observer, this looks very much like the sort of thing that the Council was looking for when it decreed: 'The rite of the Mass is to be revised in such a way that the intrinsic nature and purpose of its several parts, as also the connection between them, may be more clearly manifested, and that devout and active participation by the faithful may be more easily achieved' (§50). That is to say, it represented a more streamlined version of the existing Mass, providing much greater scope for the people's participation in the vernacular, while largely keeping the shape and feel of the original. It was, moreover, a 'Mass of Vatican II' in the double sense that it was both a fruit *of* the Council and, throughout 1965's Fourth Session, was celebrated *at* it. In fact, this was only an interim measure, prior to a much more substantially revised Order of Mass, accompanied by a wider-ranging Lectionary of scriptural readings and revamped Calendar (both items on the Fathers' wish list: §§51, 107), promulgated by Pope Paul VI in 1969. It is this *Novus Ordo*

('New Order'), which the vast majority of today's Catholics know simply as 'the Mass', that is normally, and most naturally, seen as representing the full fruit of the liturgical reform(s) initiated by Vatican II.

Interpretations and implementations

Writing in the mid-1980s, the Archbishop of Karachi (Pakistan), Cardinal Joseph Cordeiro, judged that the 'average' Catholic had 'been through a revolution in his mode of worship' since Vatican II—so much, indeed, that if shown a side-by-side comparison of 'his comings and doings and goings at' Sunday Masses in the early 1960s and the mid-1980s 'he would probably be startled out of his wits'. One need not agree with Cordeiro's overall assessment to admit that, whether a 'revolution' or not, a very great deal changed, and changed fast. Furthermore, there was not One Big Change in the sense of a single decisive watershed between 'pre-' and 'post-conciliar' liturgy. Rather there was a long period of near-constant changes, issuing both from *above* in the form of directives, recommendations, and revised texts and translations, and bubbling up from *below* as individual priests and parish liturgy committees felt sufficiently empowered to pursue their own instincts as to what might be 'pastorally efficacious to the fullest degree'. Happening in parallel to these changes in 'the ritual forms' (§49), a whole host of auxiliary adaptations, with varying degrees of official mandate, were happening around them: altars replaced, rails removed, tabernacles transplanted, vestments redesigned, art modernized, the Body of Christ received in the hand, and the Blood of Christ received at all. Try as they might, bishops often struggled to keep up with, and control, the various 'experiments' being tried in their own dioceses. (Incidentally, the latter was not only a feature in Europe and North America, as is sometimes thought. As early as May 1965, Bishop McCauley of Fort Portal, Uganda, felt the need to make the following plea: 'All changes *must* first be promulgated by the Bishop... Priests *may not* put into practice on their own initiative changes which they find in newspapers or reviews which may be duly promulgated in other countries.') By the time things had begun settling down to a more narrow palate of liturgical 'new normals' in the 1970s, it would be surprising if a lot of people, clergy and laity alike, weren't suffering from what management theorists term 'change fatigue'.

The full, global reception of the liturgical reforms is huge and complex, so we can do no more here than flag up a few main points. The most important is that the speed and enthusiasm with which *Sacrosanctum Concilium*'s several 'permissions' were taken up—most obviously those concerning vernacular languages and musical styles—rather suggests that there was a great deal of latent demand, and indeed a widespread agreement that the status quo was in need of some renewing. The invitation to explore 'legitimate variations and adaptations to different groups, regions, and peoples, especially in mission territories' was widely accepted, and many such programmes of 'inculturation' have proven successful. (Even if, in some places, the question of '*whose* vernacular?' has not always had easy answers. During the Council itself, students in Tamil-majority Chennai, India, went on hunger strike to oppose plans to introduce Masses in Hindi. Meanwhile in Kannada-majority Bangalore, liturgical favouring of Tamil has fuelled ethnic strife down to the present—occasionally erupting into violence, and even murder.) Viewed as a whole, the Council's encouragement of local customization has plausibly contributed to the Church's flourishing in much of the world, as visitors to (say) a packed, standing-room-only Tagalog Mass in the middle of a Manila shopping mall can readily appreciate.

Yet elsewhere, not least in many of the European countries whose bishops and *periti* were most influential at the Council (e.g. France, Belgium, Germany), plus in places like the USA, Canada, and Australia, Mass numbers started a sharp decline around, or soon after, the end of the Council. (To give a single example: in England and Wales, Sunday Mass attendance was

In view of the speed, rare in the Church, with which these changes have been carried out in all countries, it is difficult to avoid the fear that some measures may bring unforeseen or unhappy consequences. It is thus with devotion to the Blessed Sacrament and devotion to the Virgin Mary and the saints, whose statues have been banished from many churches...; the meet and proper ordering of the house of God, which has become a house of men...; the truly divine beauty of the Latin chants, which are now banned...

Must we, however, conclude from these considerations that all these things should have been kept unchanged? The Council, with temperance and prudence, has answered otherwise. Some reform and renewal was needed.

Marcel Lefebvre CSSp (1905–91), pastoral letter, 6 June 1965

Superior-General of Congregation of the Holy Ghost, 1962–8, and formerly Archbishop of Dakar (Senegal); founded Society of St Pius X in 1970; excommunicated under Pope John Paul II in 1988

2.1 million in 1965, 1.8 million in 1975, and 1.5 million in 1985. By 2019, on the eve of the pandemic, it was 0.7 million.) Certainly, cause-and-effect is not always easy to ascertain, and plenty else has been 'going on' in both the Church and the wider world throughout this period. Worth remembering, too, is the fact that pastoral problems were already evident in some of these countries before the Council, and were part of the reasons why it was called in the first place. Nevertheless, a large part of the reforms' explicit *raison d'être* was precisely to equip the Church to meet such challenges. At a minimum, it is reasonable to ask if their implementation has yet attained the level of 'pastorally efficacious to the fullest degree'.

Chapter 5

Dei Verbum and divine revelation

'Hearing the word of God with reverence and proclaiming it with faith, the sacred synod takes its direction from these words of St. John: "We announce to you the eternal life which dwelt with the Father and was made visible to us. What we have seen and heard we announce to you, so that you may have fellowship with us and our common fellowship be with the Father and His Son Jesus Christ" (1 John 1:2–3).' Thus begins Vatican II's Dogmatic Constitution on Divine Revelation, called *Dei Verbum* ('the word of God'). After affirming Vatican II's continuity with the councils of Trent and Vatican I, *Dei Verbum*'s first article closes by stating its intention 'to set forth authentic doctrine on divine revelation and how it is handed on, so that by hearing the message of salvation the whole world may believe, by believing it may hope, and by hoping it may love'. This brief preface indicates several important commitments, chief among them an ecclesial orientation that is missional (that 'the whole world may believe'), dialogical, and otherwise *ad extra*; that is, focused outward. The Church, according to *Dei Verbum*, announces a message it has been given by God through Jesus. This message leads to a common fellowship of salvation, to hope, and to love. Evangelization is central, and an ecclesiology is hinted at (developed in other Council documents) that focuses on *listening* to the work of the Holy Spirit at all levels of the Church, and to dialogue with non-Catholic Christians and with the non-Christian world.

While *Dei Verbum* may still inspire and edify, most of the affirmations in it, taken by themselves, seem rather unremarkable today: Jesus Christ is, of course, the centre of the Catholic faith; reading and studying the Bible in the vernacular is, of course, vital for the Christian spiritual life. Indeed, compared to some other well-known Vatican II documents, the historical and theological importance of *Dei Verbum* can hide in plain view. The document was not tackling a specific neuralgic issue head on, like religious liberty or the relationship between the pope and the bishops. Nevertheless, understanding *Dei Verbum* is crucial for understanding Vatican II, both as a historical event and as a corpus of texts. Frequently cited among Vatican II's greatest achievements was a new scriptural focus it engendered in all areas of Catholic life and thought, from the liturgy and personal devotion to a reinvigoration of biblical criticism and theology. The early debates in 1962 that ultimately led to *Dei Verbum* propelled the Council forward in a reformist orientation and a style that both saturated the final texts and came to encapsulate the ethos or spirit of the Council. For these reasons and others, a case can be made that *Dei Verbum* is the fundamental document of the Council.

Ressourcement: the triumph of a reformist orientation

While there are important affirmations in the text—stances taken, certain paths trod instead of others, subtle corrections of past views—*Dei Verbum* is most significant for its reform of *style*. In this sense, the medium was, in a very real way, the message. The Constitution on Divine Revelation evidenced a rather stark discontinuity with the reigning neo-scholastic method and tone that had dominated official Catholic teaching documents and clerical education since the 19th century. *Dei Verbum* can be seen

> The Council faced a more difficult situation when, on the same day, the schema dealing with 'the sources of revelation' was presented to the Fathers. The text was, if one may use the label, utterly a product of the 'anti-Modernist' mentality that had taken shape about the turn of the century. The text was written in a spirit of condemnation and negation which, in contrast with the great positive initiative of the liturgy schema, had a frigid and even offensive tone to many of the Fathers...
>
> The same cramped thinking, once so necessary as a line of defense, impregnated the text and informed it with a theology of negations and prohibitions; although in themselves they might well have been valid, they certainly could not produce the positive note which was now to be expected from the Council.
>
> **Joseph Ratzinger (1927–)**, writing in 1966
>
> German theologian and *peritus* to Cardinal Frings, Archbishop of Cologne; Pope Benedict XVI, 2005–13

as a kind of official canonization of the *ressourcement* movements (biblical, liturgical, patristic) which gained momentum in the decades leading up to the Council. Drawing on this theological scholarship and pastoral energy, the Council Fathers and their expert assistants reached deep into the past to recover biblical and patristic language and modes of thought. Paradoxically, this turn to the oldest sources ushered in the new: specifically, a 'new view of the phenomenon of tradition', in the words of the young German professor, Joseph Ratzinger. The future pope was, alongside Yves Congar, one of *Dei Verbum*'s chief architects.

In the course of the First Session, it became clear that a group of Council Fathers, of whom Cardinal Ottaviani was seen as a natural head, wanted Vatican II to confirm the status quo and clearly condemn a variety of modern 'errors' in the vein of Pius IX's *Syllabus of Errors* (1864). Ideally, this would be done fairly quickly and certainly without any unseemly amount of public argument. In rejecting the original draft text on Revelation, the Majority asserted that they did not come to Rome just to rubber-stamp pre-approved neo-scholastic documents. This early debate over the style and content of a document teaching the most fundamental Catholic beliefs helped the Majority find its feet. The reformist orientation that emerged set the tone for a number of later debates at the Council, for example concerning religious liberty, ecumenism, the Jewish people, and ecclesiology.

The 'source' of divine revelation: Jesus of Nazareth

The most important affirmation of *Dei Verbum* is that God's revelation to humanity is not, first and foremost, a list of doctrinal and moral teachings found in the Bible or the tradition of the Church. Rather, the fullness of revelation is the *person* of Jesus Christ (§7). The foundational event of the Christian life and the Catholic Church's *raison d'être* is an encounter with Jesus of Nazareth. This new articulation, albeit of an ancient truth, did not diminish doctrine or tradition (much less scripture), but put the emphasis on what all these things ultimately point to: the person of Christ. Along with this emphasis came a shift towards a personalistic approach to revelation: God unfolds God's self-communication to all of humanity, culminating in His Son. God's creatures respond personally and communally to the divine initiative with faith, prayer, good works, and worship. This personalistic approach constitutes an option different from a neo-scholastic starting point which saw the special revelation of the gospel as a 'new law' (*nova lex*) which supplemented and enhanced the universally accessible foundation of 'natural theology'. *Dei Verbum*'s view of Christ and revelation was also influenced by the 20th-century rise of a more explicitly evangelical 'kerygmatic Christology' associated with *ressourcement* reformers like Romano Guardini (the *kerygma* is the central gospel message). This re-presentation of God's revelation through the person of Jesus was a boon for the Christocentric dynamism apparent in other conciliar documents like *Gaudium et Spes*. It served as a touchstone for the reformist energy of the Council as a whole.

Ressourcement and a thorny old issue: scripture and tradition

Leading up to Vatican II, Catholic theologians had begun to revisit old debates—what is the precise relationship between scripture and tradition? What is the nature of tradition? There was not one unanimous Catholic position to these complex questions before the Reformation. During the 16th century, both questions proved to be signs of contradiction between Protestants and Catholics. The context in which Martin Luther first developed the foundational Protestant commitment to *sola scriptura* (scripture alone) should be remembered: it was only after Luther's debate opponent, the sharp Catholic professor Johann Eck, convinced Luther during the Leipzig Disputation in 1519 that his views were incompatible with some teachings of the ecumenical Council of Constance (1414–18). Thus, for Catholics, the legacy of the Protestant enshrinement of the Bible implied a rejection of tradition, including the teachings of popes and ecumenical councils, the mechanisms for resolving interminable doctrinal disputes and enacting disciplinary reform.

The Council of Trent, which met to try to stem the tide of the Reformation, condemned Luther's *sola scriptura*. Saying 'no' to Luther's conception was one thing. But the bishops and theologians at Trent realized that Catholics were not all on the same page about how to *positively* explain the relationship between scripture and tradition. And, they asked, what exactly was the difference between 'Tradition' and 'traditions'? The category seemed to include special practices—in, say, liturgy, church discipline, and piety—but also fundamental doctrinal commitments concerning Christ, the Trinity, and the sacraments.

One of the oldest Catholic views of 'tradition' saw it primarily in authoritative commentary on scripture, which was considered 'materially' sufficient (but not 'formally'). This position long pre-dated Protestantism.

When the draft of a decree at the Council of Trent claimed that God's revelation was contained 'partly' in scripture and 'partly' in tradition (the famous *partim-partim* formula), a handful of Council Fathers complained. Didn't such a formula denigrate scripture as somehow lacking necessary content? The great majority seemed not to have thought so, but they were willing to change the formula in order not to scandalize anyone. Unanimity was the ideal, whenever possible—a constant at Catholic ecumenical councils down the centuries. And so the word 'partly' was deleted from the final Tridentine decree, and revelation was said to be transmitted via 'the written books [the Bible] and the unwritten traditions'.

In the debates before Vatican II, some Catholic theologians wanted to revisit this issue. They thought Catholic teaching had drifted too far into a static 'two sources' position that actually went well beyond Trent's careful final formulation. This gave the unhappy impression that the Catholic Church saw scripture and tradition as two treasure chests of revelation, containing discrete data and ideas. In this understanding, for the fullness of Catholic truth, one needed both treasure chests—and Protestants had only one (this was an important plank in centuries of anti-Protestant polemic and apologetic strategy).

At Vatican II, the Theological Commission's schema *De Fontibus* explicitly included two-source language, as if this position was settled Catholic doctrine. Removing this language was considered a great success for the growing number of Council Fathers who wished for a document that was more historically conscious, personalistic, and ecumenically sensitive; many of these Fathers also sought to avoid the persistent charge that Catholicism

There was solemn and long disputation
on the founts of divine Revelation;
  there used to be two,
  but when under review,
they have suffered a grave mutilation.

John O'Loughlin (1911–85), limerick composed during Council

Bishop of Darwin (Australia), 1949–85

Diuturna de Revelatione
peracta iam disceptatione,
  eius fontes olim bina,
  recognita, in fine
Obscurantur, heu! confusione.

Bernard Wall (1894–1976), Latin translation of above

Bishop of Brentwood (England), 1955–69

subordinated scripture to tradition or the magisterium. They felt that the 'two-source' formulation in *De Fontibus* was ossifying at best and canonizing a false theory at worst.

Ultimately, *Dei Verbum* handled the thorny issue of 'sources' expertly and sensitively. Article 10 of the Constitution teaches that scripture and tradition are both entrusted to the Church and together form 'one sacred deposit' of the Word of God. Neither scripture nor tradition was called a 'source' (Trent used the Latin word *fons*) in its own right. *Dei Verbum* pivoted to a new formula: 'Hence there exists a close connection and communication between sacred tradition and Sacred Scripture. For both of them, flowing from the same divine wellspring [*scaturigine*, not *fons*], in a certain way merge into a unity and tend toward the same end.' The Council Fathers had successfully revisited an old controversy and settled it, without making clear winners and losers on the old terms of the debate. *Dei Verbum* refocused attention onto the person of Christ as *the* source, avoiding taking a stance on the one-source (scripture, interpreted through tradition) and two-source (scripture and tradition) positions. In the drafting of *Dei Verbum*, *ressourcement* theologians contributed to the 'sources' debate with this very deft move that underscored the Council's desire for Christocentricism, an ecumenical approach, and language that better reflected the deepest tradition of the Church rather than the reactive formulations of the Counter-Reformation, however legitimate they may have been in their original context.

The *ressourcement* theologians behind *Dei Verbum* were influenced by Romanticism, Newman's theory of doctrinal development, personalist philosophy, and even Karl Barth, one of the greatest Protestant theologians of the day. The ghosts of Luther and Calvin, rather than functioning merely as bogeymen, were being parleyed with critically and respectfully, in a manner true to Catholic tradition but open to an ecumenical future.

Development of doctrine: an emerging historical consciousness

Dei Verbum gave further impetus to Vatican II's reformist orientation by explicitly teaching that doctrine develops. In the wake of the Protestant Reformation, the idea that doctrine could develop—which is, after all, a form of *change*—was widely rejected by Catholics. The Church's faith was the faith Jesus had, once for all, given to the apostles, who then handed down that deposit to their successors, 'transmitted as it were from hand to hand', as Trent taught. The idea that Catholic doctrine (even practices in some circumstances) could change or develop was especially antithetical to the Jansenist and Gallican schools. They brandished the immutability of Catholicism as a weapon against the alleged amoeba-like nature of Protestantism. Jansenists and Gallicans also appealed to immutability and antiquity to resist the expanding claims of the papacy, and the theology of ultramontanists like the Jesuits.

But by the time of Vatican II, Catholic theologians had virtually all come to accept that doctrine did indeed develop, though there were different explanations for how this occurred. Because of the work of the brilliant Anglican convert John Henry Newman (1801–90) and some other figures, the concept of doctrinal development had become the established way of explaining the existence and coherence of important Catholic beliefs that were not explicit in scripture or the earliest Christian sources. The formal dogmatic definitions of the Virgin Mary's Immaculate (sinless) Conception in 1854 and her 'Assumption' into heaven in 1950 form an important backdrop to a climate of increased Catholic reflection on doctrinal development, not to mention Vatican I's definition in 1870 of the pope's authority to make such infallible declarations at all, a prerogative that was widely disputed well into the 1800s.

Dei Verbum canonized no particular theory of *how* doctrinal development actually happens, although the pivotal article (§8) was clearly reliant on Congar, who depended on Cardinal Newman (made a saint in 2019, Newman enjoys a quasi-official pride of place surrounding these questions). According to §8, 'the tradition which comes from the Apostles develops (*proficit*) in the Church with the help of the Holy Spirit'. This doctrinal development occurs through 'contemplation and study', through the 'penetrating understanding' that experience brings, and through the preaching and teaching of bishops. All believers who pray have a role to play in this process: citations of Luke 2:19 and 51 cast a contemplative, Marian tone. Development is a means by which 'the Church constantly moves forward toward the fullness of divine truth'. The ecclesiology implied here squares with *Lumen Gentium*'s image of a 'pilgrim church'. Recognizing the reality of doctrinal development and sketching it in a basically Newmanian manner was one of *Dei Verbum*'s most important contributions for the future of Catholic theology. This recognition was a result of theologians' more organic understandings of the phenomenon of tradition, as well as accepting the hard facts of history that scholars had grappled with through critical study dating back to the Enlightenment era and even, in more limited ways, to Renaissance humanism.

This formal acceptance at Vatican II of the idea that doctrine can develop and the Church can grow in understanding God's revelation was essential grounding for numerous teachings of the Council. The most striking example of doctrinal development occurred when Vatican II amended church teaching regarding religious liberty. *Dignitatis Humanae*, in fact, used a more explicit 'change word' (*evolvere*) to denote development than did *Dei Verbum* (*proficere* could be translated 'to advance' or 'make progress'). *Dei Verbum* imparted a view of tradition as a living hermeneutic that norms ecclesial life, and a growing understanding of the gospel and the Christian journey. This view allows for a more robust reformist orientation than when tradition is seen mainly as information—as discrete doctrinal data that had been literally, some even thought orally, passed down through a (historically dubious) chain of unbroken witnesses.

A more scriptural Church: *Dei Verbum*'s *aggiornamento*

The Constitution on the Liturgy's (*Sacrosanctum Concilium*) emphasis on scripture's role in worship (§§7, 21, 34, 55) coupled with *Dei Verbum*'s exhortations regarding lay Bible reading (§§21–6) serve as the crowning achievements of the 20th-century biblical movement in the Catholic Church. *Dei Verbum* also declared that the magisterium—that is, the formal teaching authority of the Church—is 'not above the Word of God but serves it' (§10). This would, of course, never have been denied in Catholic theology. However, making the subservience of the magisterium to the Word of God crystal clear was important for ecumenical and ecclesiological reasons.

We have already seen that *Dei Verbum* avoided competitive language when speaking of scripture and tradition, ultimately subordinating both to the person of Jesus, who is himself the fullness of God's revelation. Nevertheless, *Dei Verbum* accords to scripture what might be called a prima facie primacy. This primacy (firstness) is not a supremacy over, much less against, tradition; rather, it presupposes harmony and organic mutuality with tradition. But a special exaltation of scripture in the document is clear. Indeed, it was a feared denigration or marginalization of 'Tradition'—the bulwark against Protestantism and against undesirable 'innovation' or 'novelty' within Catholicism—that drove many of the Minority's critiques of *Dei Verbum*. The remarkable statement that the Church venerates scripture 'just as she venerates the body of the Lord' (§21) certainly suggests the normativity of the biblical witness. Through the Bible, especially its public proclamation in the liturgy, *Dei Verbum* teaches that the faithful come into contact with Christ in a way that is analogous to the Real Presence of Jesus in the Eucharist (§21). The structure of the document itself suggests a prima facie scriptural primacy—the final 16 articles (of 26 total) are concerned exclusively with the Bible, and the first 10 articles consider scripture and tradition more or less concurrently.

The vision of *Dei Verbum* is for personal contact with scripture in the liturgy and through (vernacular) Bible reading: the faithful are encouraged to turn directly to the Bible for spiritual nourishment and religious instruction (§22, 25). Expanding the avenues opened up by Pius XII in *Divino Afflante Spiritu* (1943), contemporary means of critical biblical scholarship are encouraged (§23). Against the serious warnings of members of the Minority like Cardinal Ernesto Ruffini of Palermo, who held to a strict view of biblical inerrancy and literalistic interpretations of the Genesis story, the Majority prevailed in applying inerrancy (teaching *sine errore*; 'without error') not to all historical or scientific content in scripture, but to 'that truth which God wanted put into sacred writings for the sake of salvation' (§11). Catholic biblical scholarship had finally overcome the persistent ghost of Modernism and the clampdown on critical biblical scholarship. However, the Constitution was very clear that neither private scriptural interpretation nor historical-critical exegesis have the final determinative say in teaching Catholic doctrine (§23).

The last six articles teach that the prayerful study of scripture is of paramount importance not just for preaching clergy but for all Christians, since 'ignorance of the Scriptures is ignorance of Christ' (§25, quoting St Jerome's famous statement). While it is a myth that lay people were not encouraged to read the Bible until Vatican II, it is undeniable that *Dei Verbum* placed an emphasis on personal scripture reading and study that was unprecedented in post-Tridentine Catholicism. This emphasis has been deepened by postconciliar movements, by changing parish and devotional cultures, and by manifold writings of recent popes, bishops, and other leading Catholic figures. In light of diverse and ambiguous (if not outright negative) late medieval and early modern Catholic approaches to vernacular Bible reading by the laity, *Dei Verbum*'s affirmations evidence a stunning development in Catholic thought and practice, though a development that was long in the making.

A comparison of the status quo even in the early 20th century to contemporary Catholic attitudes on Bible reading reveals a striking difference—from popes to priests to the parish leaders and campus ministers who, in some places, work hard to sign up as many people in the pews as possible for Bible studies that are often lay led. This is not to mention the gulf separating *Dei Verbum* from the cautious and even prohibitive policies reflected in some early modern magisterial documents. Pope Clement XI's

4. The Council Aula (i.e. 'Hall') occupying the central nave of St Peter's Basilica.

Unigenitus of 1713 (see the notorious articles 79–86) *condemned* ideas that read like they could be taken from *Dei Verbum* or the writings of a modern pope. An ecumenical council implying that one will have a deficient understanding of Christ without sufficient personal contact with the scriptures is a remarkable reform. A desire for a more scriptural church at every level is ultimately a claim not just about revelation but about ecclesiology. How the Catholic Church understands itself and its mission—probably the central theme of Vatican II—is the subject of the next chapter.

Chapter 6
Ecclesiology: the nature of the Church

It is for good reason that Vatican II has been called an ecclesiological council. Previous ecumenical councils certainly worked with assumed theologies of the Church ('ecclesiologies'), especially insofar as they published slews of ecclesiastical policies and norms seeking to reform or otherwise improve Catholic life. Previous councils also issued numerous teachings and regulations *relevant* to ecclesiology, that is, to the nature and mission of the Church. Seeking to present a united front to a fractured Europe, the Council of Trent purposely avoided some of the most divisive ecclesiological issues of the day. Vatican I, of course, defined dogma regarding the nature of the papal office (notably infallibility) but had little to say about the rest of the Church. Vatican II, then, was actually the first council to really tackle ecclesiology head on, in a holistic and even systematic manner. In the Dogmatic Constitution *Lumen Gentium*, Vatican II contributed an ecclesiological teaching document that was remarkably multifaceted and far-reaching, while retaining a sense of cohesion and accessibility.

Lumen Gentium was promulgated on 21 November 1964. Its serene, warm, and at times majestic language masks the compromises and painful birth-pangs from which it emerged. The difficult debates over the nature and mission of the Church were exhausting, and at times heated, but they were not in vain.

Not only did the Council Fathers boldly address pressing contemporary concerns and issues, they produced a kind of charter document that was suffused with scripture, rooted in tradition, and applicable beyond its day. This Dogmatic Constitution by no means answered all the questions, but it did point a way forward on a number of issues. Other documents, issued separately, expanded upon these opened paths. These include *Christus Dominus*, on the office of bishop; *Unitatis Redintegratio*, on ecumenism; *Dignitatis Humanae*, on religious liberty; *Gaudium et Spes*, on the Church and the world; *Nostra Aetate*, on the Jews and on world religions; and *Ad Gentes*, on missionary work. We will consider the first three in this chapter, and the next three in Chapter 7. One could make the case that *Lumen Gentium* is the key document of the Council, since it served as the foundation of so many other texts covering myriad important themes. The language of *Lumen Gentium* became not only the emphasis of many other Vatican II texts—'People of God', 'ecumenism', 'pilgrim Church', 'collegiality', 'lay apostolate', 'universal call to holiness'—but also inspired many postconciliar initiatives and ideas that attempted to capture the 'spirit' of the Council.

A Christocentric and *ad extra* Church

Let us begin with some overarching themes addressed in *Lumen Gentium*. The Constitution begins with a simple sentence: 'Christ is the Light of nations' (§1). The eponymous '*Lumen*', then, is not the Church, but Jesus. In this fundamental Christocentrism *Lumen Gentium* picks up where the framers of *Dei Verbum* left off—with divine revelation reconceived as a narrative of life-giving and redeeming relationship, centred around a *person*. Christocentrism is basic to the Catholic tradition, but the Council Fathers also had ecumenism in mind when, in the process of redrafting, they made 'the light' refer to Christ rather than the Church. They meant to dispel persistent perceptions or (mis) understandings commonly held by some other Christians: that rather than Jesus, Catholicism was really all about the pope, or the Virgin Mary and the saints, or institutional expansion and power. In addition to buttressing the Christocentric and ecumenical tones already set at the Council, *Lumen Gentium* sought to forge an ecclesiology that was *evangelical* and *ad extra*. By 'evangelical' we mean a Church that is preoccupied not with itself but with spreading the gospel, the Good News of the imminence of God's Kingdom and salvation in Jesus Christ. A Church that is oriented *ad extra* is facing outward, not inward. The Council's (and thus, the Church's) evangelical mission is simply the logical consequence of the fact that Jesus is the light of the world (§1). This is why *Lumen Gentium* addresses not only other Christians, but also non-Christians and the world at large, including non-believers.

An ecclesiology of 'mystery'

Lumen Gentium's first chapter expounds upon the Church as 'mystery' (note that *sacramentum* and *mysterium* have overlapping meanings in Latin), as the receiver of the revelation of God and hence the *locus* of divine love and grace. Before any discussion of offices, authority, or roles (clerical or otherwise) the Council considers the story of redemption in Christ, a story which the Church is called to embody and extend throughout the world. A key passage in §8 closes chapter one, where a very delicate balance is struck between the visible, external elements of the Church and the invisible, spiritual realities:

> This Church [the 'one Church of Christ'] constituted and organized in the world as a society, subsists in [*subsistit in*] the Catholic Church, which is governed by the successor of Peter [the pope] and by the Bishops in communion with him, although many elements of sanctification and of truth are found outside of its visible structure. These elements, as gifts belonging to the Church of Christ, are forces impelling toward catholic unity.

This passage doctrinally undergirds Vatican II's shift to a positive embrace of non-Catholic Christians as brothers and sisters in Christ rather than schismatics and heretics. Only two decades before, Pope Pius XII expressed direct identification between the Roman Catholic Church and the One Church of Christ: 'the true Church of Jesus Christ *is* the One, Holy, Catholic, Apostolic and Roman Church' (encyclical letter *Mystici Corporis Christi* §13, emphasis added). This language was present in earlier drafts of *De Ecclesia*, but eventually changed to this 'subsists in' formula.

Why did the majority of the Council Fathers prefer the somewhat odd, technical language that the Church of Christ *subsistit in* the Catholic Church? One could gloss *Lumen Gentium* 8 to say: 'the church founded by Christ continues to exist fully [subsists] in the Catholic Church'. The delicate 'both-and' dynamic that such a statement suggests encapsulates Vatican II-style ecumenism. Traditional claims are not repudiated or backtracked on—the Church is described as a visible *societas*, not an invisible body of believers or a panoply of denominations; the fullness of the Church of Christ is present only in those Churches headed by bishops in full communion with the pope. Nevertheless, the *subsistit in* formulation allowed for the formal recognition of the many truly Christian and truly ecclesial realities present in non-Catholic communities, ranging from the ancient Orthodox Churches to the major Churches of the Reformation to the newest or smallest sect of evangelical or charismatic Christians. These positive realities are to be celebrated and cultivated, as 'forces impelling towards' that 'catholic unity' willed by Christ and desired by the ecumenical movement. This ecclesiological shift opened the way to the positive affirmations later in *Lumen Gentium* and in *Unitatis Redintegratio*.

The People of God and the lay vocation

One of the most remarked upon decisions of the entire Council was the placing of *Lumen Gentium* chapter two, on the 'People of

God', before chapter three, which concerns the ecclesiastical hierarchy and its authority. This redactional choice was a symbolic statement that the hierarchy is part of the People of God rather than something separate from or above it. This has at times been misinterpreted as an assertion of the priority of the laity over the ordained (it is the laity who, after all, make up the overwhelming majority of the Church). Priests and bishops would thus be reconceived as delegates of the laity, and therefore only possessing delegated authority. Indeed, this was the exact fear of Bishop Eduardo Martínez Gonzáles of Zamora (Spain), who in October 1963 spoke out against rearranging the chapters in this way. The hierarchy, argued this bishop of the Minority, are 'ontologically' and logically *prior* to the People of God. They generate the laity, and not vice versa, and thus there is an 'inequality' between them. The Council, Martínez Gonzáles warned, should be careful not to foster democratic ideas that are alien to Catholic ecclesiology.

To the conciliar Majority, such concerns revealed fundamental ecclesiological misunderstandings. *Lumen Gentium* chapter two presented the Church as a people united in Christ through common faith and baptism. There is, then, a fundamental theological *equality* in baptism, before distinctions were made as to sacraments, offices, and duties—distinctions which all affirmed were objective, appropriate, and necessary. By positioning *all* the baptized as the People of God, the Council Fathers of the Majority were not attempting a revolutionary inverting of the hierarchical pyramid; rather, they wanted to shift away from such an image entirely, and towards privileging organic images of the Church as a body, a people, a community of all the faithful—whether ordained clergy, laity, or religious.

Nevertheless, critics such as Martínez Gonzáles had put their finger squarely on a number of challenging issues. *Ressourcement*-guided theologians and pastors could and did cite biblical and early Church precedent for a robust ecclesiology of the baptized: for a laity with real agency, who actively participate in liturgy and actively collaborate with their clergy in the internal and external affairs of the Church. But as Martínez Gonzáles and others were obviously aware, Vatican II was also signalling, in some cases eagerly and hopefully, to contemporary societal, cultural, and political developments. Many Catholics saw these developments in a positive light, but not all. In a post-Second World War landscape where democracy triumphed in North America and much of Europe, decolonization was accelerating in Africa and Asia, and a powerful social Catholicism was awakening in South America, *aggiornamento* meant the baptizing of certain ecclesio-political emphases that were at the very least in tension with the ideals of a man like Martínez Gonzáles, who hailed from Generalissimo Franco's Spain. The counter-revolutionary and counter-Enlightenment narratives that had so marked post-1789 Catholicism were still taken for granted in certain sectors of the Church—if not as achievable realities, at least as abstract 'ideals' that could never be abandoned on the level of principle. At the Council, these political and cultural tensions lurked in the background of many ecclesiological discussions. They came to a head in the debate over the document on religious liberty, which was in some ways the long-delayed baptism of the post-1789 modern liberal state.

Despite tensions and controversies, some of the fruits of *Lumen Gentium*'s teaching on the Church seem to have been broadly 'received' by Catholics, then and now, in a more or less unambiguously positive fashion. Chapter five, concerning 'the Universal Call to Holiness', presents a profound vision for an emboldened People of God, enlivened by the Holy Spirit, where different but compatible vocations are lived out for the glory of God. Postconciliar reception of this vision has occurred in more politically and theologically 'conservative' circles (e.g. Opus Dei), more 'progressive' ones (e.g. Liberation Theology), and in movements that defy easy categorization, like the charismatic renewal. Common ground is found in a widespread embrace of Vatican II's 'epideictic' language concerning vocation.

Epideictic refers to a genre of rhetoric that exhorts and inspires through praise. This style predominates in many of the documents, not least in *Lumen Gentium*'s admonitions on the universal call to holiness. The emphasis postconciliar Catholicism places on the unique vocations of married and single lay life and on the significance and goodness of lay leadership in business, politics, the arts, social justice, and education is a happy fruit of Vatican II's ecclesiology, which was itself building on decades of Catholic reflection and action by laity and clergy. The underappreciated Decree *Apostolicam Actuositatem* envisioned an 'intensification' of the lay vocation, grounded in *Lumen Gentium*'s teaching that the laity share in the threefold office of Christ (prophet, priest, and king) through their baptism.

Episcopal collegiality: a shibboleth for re-conceiving the Church

Although not as immediately tangible as the liturgical reforms proved to be, Vatican II's ecclesiological reform was profound. The Council Fathers staged another chapter in the bitter and complicated struggle, stretching back at least to the High Middle Ages, over defining the precise relation between, on one hand, the spiritual and juridical primacy of the pope and his administrative centre (the Roman Curia), and, on the other, the authority of bishops in their respective dioceses as well as in the collective unity of the episcopate. While John XXIII originally intended Vatican II to be primarily pastoral, it quickly tackled doctrinal issues as well. The Fathers became more and more frank about addressing certain elephants in the room. One such elephant was the need, in the words of Jared Wicks, 'to remedy Vatican I's one-sided legacy on papal primacy isolated from the episcopate'. In these and other ways, Vatican II, especially in *Lumen Gentium*, 'harvest[ed] the rich growth of theology concerning the Church from 1920 to 1960'.

Strictly speaking, episcopal collegiality referred to the bishops' co-governance of the Catholic Church with the pope. No one disputed that bishops had 'ordinary and immediate' authority to sanctify, teach, and govern in their own dioceses. Everyone also accepted that the pope's primacy ('firstness') was *de iure divino*—that is, that the Roman papacy was willed by God. No one argued that the papacy was just an *ecclesiastical* (man-made and thus potentially changeable) structure of the Church, however important, like the existence and role of the College of Cardinals. But most of the bishops and their *periti* also believed that the deepest tradition of the Church—rooted ultimately in the Church Fathers and the New Testament—did not conceive of bishops as merely delegates or, put crudely, 'branch managers' of head office in Rome. Rather, they were Successors of the Apostles who received their apostolic authority directly from Christ, not from the pope.

Episcopal collegiality had become a shibboleth for a new conception of church life and governance, a conception that the Majority would argue was *retrieved* and therefore actually *more* traditional. In this vision, the pope, while certainly the head of the Church on earth, would no longer be conceived of in monarchical terms, or at least not primarily so. The pope's role, ordinarily, was to be a servant of unity (the 'servant of the servants of God', according to one ancient title). Everyone agreed, moreover, that as Successor of St Peter he had the right to intervene directly in emergencies or extreme cases. Logically, any re-conception of the relationship between the pope and the bishops should, it was thought, also change the role of the Roman Curia—this possibility simmered under the surface and sometimes erupted. The Minority, already suspicious from the *De Fontibus* debates in session one, worried that collegiality—which virtually everyone agreed *could* have an orthodox meaning—was really a Trojan Horse that, at best, undercut papal primacy. At worst, they feared it could lead to a kind of 'Modernist' democratization of the Church or a devolution into Protestant or Jansenist episcopalianism. Opponents of collegiality, like the Italian bishop Luigi Carli, evoked these 'ghosts' of the past with skill.

The turning point in this lengthy, charged, and tedious debate was a vote taken during the Second Session, on 30 October 1963. The bishops were asked to affirm or deny five questions connected to collegiality. Such votes would determine the broader debate over what shape *Lumen Gentium* would take. For example, one question asked whether the document should assert that the 'College of Bishops', always in communion with the pope, enjoys 'full and supreme power over the universal church' by divine right (this meant that this authority was *not* delegated by or derived from the pope); 2,138 Council Fathers voted yes, 408 voted no. When strong majorities in favour of all five questions were announced, it became clear that the anti-collegiality position was not nearly as large as it had seemed in light of the numerous and passionate speeches and interventions by the Minority. Some proposals were essentially non-controversial—over 98 per cent agreed that episcopacy was the 'supreme grade' of the Sacrament of Holy Orders received by priests and deacons (thus a priest was 'ordained' bishop). But opposition to some ecclesiological proposals was by no means insignificant. A full 20 per cent of the Council Fathers believed it inopportune to resurrect the 'permanent diaconate'—that is, deciding to ordain men as deacons who were not on the path to becoming priests (including, quite possibly, married men). Nevertheless, after these votes were taken it was clear that a strong statement on episcopal collegiality was the will of the great majority of the bishops at Vatican II. In the climate set by *ressourcement* theology, arguments from scripture and the early Church had a strong impact. But maybe even more importantly, the bishops had been *doing* collegial church government at the Council. As John O'Malley points out, this experience was no longer an abstraction—it was 'now part of lived reality' for about 2,500 Catholic bishops.

In a poignant reminder that ecclesiological debates virtually always have practical goals in view, Cardinal Joseph Frings (Cologne) took the floor on 8 November 1963, and berated the Holy Office. He attacked what he saw as the Curia's tendency to assume authority over the world's bishops. The applause of the assembly showed Frings's opinion was widely shared. The Archbishop of Cologne was reacting directly to a speech by Cardinal Michael Browne, an Irish Dominican and a leader in the Minority, who was introducing a companion text to *Lumen Gentium* which dealt with the authority of bishops (eventually called *Christus Dominus*). Frings's aggressive speech, written in part by Ratzinger (who would, ironically, become head of the renamed and reformed Holy Office in 1981), made a powerful argument for episcopal authority and challenged the idea that everything flowed from the pope. Frings's attack centred on the Holy Office itself, and how it was run: accusing it of unjust procedures, harming the Church, and causing scandal. Minority leaders like the Holy Office's own Ottaviani and Cardinal Giuseppe Siri of Genoa were so offended that they threatened to leave the Council if Frings did not apologize. This famous incident highlighted the intensity with which many in the Majority fought for ecclesiological reform, and the equal intensity with which many in the Minority perceived these proposed reforms as attacks not only on the papacy and the Curia, but on the Church as they knew it.

Achievements of *Lumen Gentium*

Let us look more closely at the results of these debates. Though a product of compromise and fierce dispute, *Lumen Gentium* chapter three is chock full of important doctrinal teaching, reflecting the votes on 30 October 1963 (discussed above). Article 21 taught that episcopal consecration is the fullness of the sacrament of Holy Orders. The next article affirmed that the 'college of bishops' succeeds the 'college of the Apostles'. This episcopal college, always united to the pope, possesses full and supreme power in the universal Church (§22). This affirmation is pivotal, because it means there are two locations of supreme authority in the Catholic Church: the pope and the college of bishops. The latter, however, always includes the pope, who is a member of the episcopal college and its head. Just as papal primacy is *de iure divino* (by divine right), so is episcopal authority (§24). It is not 'graciously conceded' to bishops by the pope—a point the Chilean Cardinal Raúl Silva Henríquez was keen to make. Rather, the bishops of the world receive their teaching authority from Christ, just as the bishop of Rome does. This was an important counterbalance to a mistaken view that had developed in some ultramontane circles, where the pope was seen as the fount of all authority in the Church—authority he could dispense and rescind as he saw fit.

Another closely related balancing act that *Lumen Gentium* attempted concerned understandings of infallibility. Catholics had always believed that the Church could teach certain fundamental truths of the faith with an infallibility (protection from error) guaranteed by Christ's promise to send the Holy Spirit. The victory of ultramontanism in the 19th century, however, had sometimes given the mistaken impression that this was primarily or even exclusively a prerogative of the pope. Relying on *ressourcement* methodology, *Lumen Gentium* located infallibility in the entire Church. This was another crucial scriptural and patristic recovery. Infallibility, according to the ecclesiology of *Lumen Gentium*, is first and foremost a gift to the whole believing community. Article 12 of the Constitution affirms that the People of God as a whole—the overwhelmingly majority of whom are laity—are collectively the bearers of infallibility. Papal infallibility, dogmatically defined at Vatican I, was emphatically reaffirmed. However, just as the episcopal college was recognized as the bearer of supreme authority in the Church, *Lumen Gentium* 25 teaches that not only the pope and an ecumenical council can teach infallibly, but that the bishops dispersed throughout the world can as well, when they are united in this teaching (this is the infallibility of the 'ordinary magisterium'). Precisely how such an event could be ascertained to have occurred, however, is not described and has led to much postconciliar debate, for example over highly controversial issues of moral and especially sexual teaching (such as birth control).

What about the practical day-to-day matters of running their local churches that the bishops were so concerned about? *Lumen Gentium* had dealt with the theological and sacramental foundations of the papal and episcopal offices, and the relationship between them. A separate document on the 'pastoral office of bishops' in their concrete roles in the Church was published in the Fourth Session. This Decree, *Christus Dominus*, contained a crucial passage (§8a) framing the canonical and administrative status quo for the postconciliar Church:

> To bishops, as successors of the Apostles, in the dioceses entrusted to them, there belongs per se all the ordinary, proper, and immediate authority which is required for the exercise of their pastoral office. But this never in any way infringes upon the power which the Roman pontiff has, by virtue of his office, of reserving [canonical] cases to himself or to some other authority.

This first sentence certainly reflects the collegial advances of the conciliar majority. But the second sentence's lack of any specified limit underlines the fact that, to quote O'Malley, 'the center', that is, the pope and the Roman Curia, 'never really lost control'. At least theoretically, this Roman 'center' still held all the trump cards in their relationship with the local Catholic churches of the world.

From triumphalism to dialogue: ecumenism and religious liberty

The ecclesiology of *Lumen Gentium* grounded the reformist orientations present in other documents of the Council, especially those dedicated to ecumenism and religious liberty. The Decree *Unitatis Redintegratio* is the central statement of the Council on relations with non-Catholic Christians. *Lumen Gentium* 8 (discussed above) and 15, as well as *Unitatis Redintegratio* 3, upheld traditional ecclesiological claims to Catholic uniqueness but in a manner that was inclusive, rather than exclusive.

The recognition of the existence of truly ecclesial elements outside the visible boundaries of the Catholic Church, and the assertion that these positive elements impelled towards ecclesial unity, served as the foundations for Catholic optimism about ecumenism. *Lumen Gentium* 15 even gives a list of many of these elements of goodness and truth in the various beliefs and practices of non-Catholic Christians and their communities: cherishing the sacred scriptures, sincere and zealous belief in the Triune God, recognition of baptism and other sacraments, retaining the episcopate (in certain communities), celebrating the Eucharist, cultivating devotion to Mary, fostering the life of Christian prayer, desiring ecclesial unity in the Holy Spirit, and the ultimate witness of martyrdom.

Lumen Gentium did not just indicate areas of commonality, it called for reform in how the Church's devotional and theological life is presented. One of many possible examples: it exhorted Catholics to 'assiduously keep away from whatever, either by word or deed, could lead separated brethren or any other into error regarding the true doctrine of the Church' concerning the Virgin Mary (§67). While this admonition certainly reflected the Council Fathers' understanding of 'true' Catholic devotion, they made explicit their concern that excessive or superstitious Marian devotion was an ecumenical problem as well. In one of the narrowest votes of the Council, a slight majority preferred to include teaching on the Virgin Mary as a chapter in the Constitution on the Church rather than in a separate document. The narrowly victorious position did not wish to downplay Mary's importance; they were motivated, rather, by a desire to consider the Mother of Christ *within* the Church, as the foremost disciple of Jesus.

Vatican II's commitment to ecumenism is borne out in the entire document and summarized in the introduction to *Unitatis Redintegratio*. Article 6 even acknowledged the wisdom of a principle very close to a slogan associated with the Protestant

Reformation, *Ecclesia semper reformanda* ('the Church always reforming', or 'always in need of reforming'). The critical passage contains the only instance in the entire Vatican II corpus in which the term *reformatio* is applied to the Church:

> Christ summons the Church to continual reformation (*perennem reformationem*) as she sojourns here on earth. The Church is always in need of this, in so far as she is an institution of humans here on earth. Thus if, in various times and circumstances, there have been deficiencies in moral conduct or in church discipline, or even in the way that church teaching has been formulated—to be carefully distinguished from the deposit of faith itself—these can and should be set right at the opportune moment.

While a recognition that the Church 'in so far as she is a human institution' needs reform was in no way controversial, the next clause, that this 'reformation' might extend *to the formulation of doctrine* (rather than just to morals or discipline) was a profound repudiation of Catholic triumphalism.

Vatican II turned from the negative language of 'lack' (schism, heresy) to positive language. Sanctifying and truly Christian and ecclesial 'elements' were recognized outside of (but by no means totally separate from) the visible structures of full Catholic communion. These particular developments revolutionized language more than doctrine as such. After all, Catholics had always held that anyone who was baptized was a fellow Christian in some sense—for there could only be one baptism, Triune baptism. Before the Council, Catholic teaching clearly maintained the *possibility* that a non-Catholic could be saved. Even narrow interpreters of the traditional axiom 'outside the Church there is no salvation' admitted this, at least under certain circumstances. The papacy had officially taught this possibility, explicitly so in some encyclicals of Pope Pius IX. And, in a famous incident in 1949, the Vatican's Holy Office (headed by Cardinal Ottaviani, who could hardly be accused of excessively irenic positions regarding non-Catholics) censured an American Jesuit named Leonard Feeney, whose fire-and-brimstone preaching in Boston seemed to deny any possibility that a non-Catholic could be saved without formally converting. Feeney was eventually excommunicated.

Thus, while it is a myth that before Vatican II the Catholic Church held that 'Protestants go to Hell' (at least necessarily so) the magnitude of these ecumenical developments should also not be understated. For beneath this change in language lay profound shifts in orientation, perspective, and attitude. *Lumen Gentium*'s careful formulation did not force Catholics to deny or mitigate cherished elements of internal ecclesial self-understanding. Rather, it allowed, even demanded, a departure from the exclusive and at times overwhelmingly negative language and attitudes of the past. In doing so, Vatican II opened the door for Catholics to walk together with non-Catholic Christians as brothers and sisters, a process that had already begun and received encouragement from many Christian voices, Catholic, Protestant, and Orthodox. Catholicism was late to the ecumenical party, at least officially speaking. But it arrived with a serious bang, and ecumenism became a central commitment of the postconciliar Church.

Especially when coupled with Vatican II's commitment to ecumenism, it would be difficult to overstate the significance of the Council's teaching on religious liberty. The German theologian Peter Hünermann was not exaggerating when he called the Declaration *Dignitatis Humanae* 'a decisive document in the history of humanity'. There were many reasons it was so. The ecumenical importance of proclaiming religious freedom, however, was made explicit in the lengthy and tense debates over the various drafts of *Dignitatis Humanae*. Proclaiming not pragmatic toleration but *de iure* religious liberty—that is, the position that the human person has a God-given right to civil religious freedom—was especially critical for Vatican II's *ad extra* and ecumenical focus (see article 2 especially).

Did you hear that Boston has a new auxiliary bishop? Yes? Who? Answer: Billy Graham.

Marion Forst (1910–2007), reporting a joke doing the rounds in October 1964

Bishop of Dodge City, Kansas (USA), 1960–76

The ecumenical dimension to the religious liberty debate loomed so large that a first draft text (from November 1963) was initially included as chapter five of the Decree on Ecumenism. The Italian *peritus* Pietro Pavan explained why Cardinal Bea's Secretariat for Promoting Christian Unity was so supportive of the declaration:

> Many non-Catholics are opposed to the Church or at least suspect it of Machiavellianism, because it demands freedom for itself in those political communities where Catholics are in the minority, while refusing the same freedom to non-Catholics in political communities where Catholics are in the majority. Hence it was essential for the Church to state its view on religious freedom unequivocally. Unless this was done, a larger and deeper development of the ecumenical movement would be difficult, perhaps even impossible.

Those favouring *Dignitatis Humanae* successfully argued that unless the Catholic Church clearly proclaimed its commitment to the religious liberty of those who were not members of it, ecumenical progress would be difficult or impossible. This concern for reforming Catholic teaching and practice not only for the sake of internal renewal but for the sake of those outside its visible boundaries dominated Vatican II's Fourth Session and the key documents it produced—the focus of the next chapter.

Chapter 7
Church and world

Vatican II's favoured biblical image of Christ as 'the light of the nations', which entails the Church's mission to bring 'the light of Christ to all people' (LG 1), expresses well the Council's basic orientation towards those outside it. Indeed, the first text formally issued by the Council, just two weeks into the First Session, was a short 'Message to the World', drafted by the French theologian Marie-Dominique Chenu, and described by another—the Jesuit Henri de Lubac—as 'a sort of manifesto':

> We wish to convey to all people and to all nations the message of salvation, love, and peace which Jesus Christ, son of the living God, brought to the world and entrusted to the Church…
>
> We will strive to propose to the people of our times the truth of God in its entirety and purity so that they may understand it and accept it freely…
>
> United here from every nation under heaven, we carry in our hearts the anxieties of all peoples entrusted to us, the anxieties of body and soul, sorrows and desires, and hopes. We turn our mind constantly towards all the anxieties afflicting men today…
>
> Is not this conciliar assembly—admirable for its diversity of races, nations and tongues—a testimony of a community bound by fraternal love which it bears as a visible sign?

Although now largely forgotten, it is a revealing statement of intent, and many of its themes recur throughout the more formal conciliar documents. The warm tone with which it directly addresses non-Catholics would, moreover, set a trend.

This engagement was far from a one-way street. Throughout the Council, goings-on in the world outside the Aula were constant sources of interest, influence, intrigue, and infiltration (or at least the fear of it: rumours of schemes by this or that communist government were rife throughout). Most obviously, major world events could hardly fail to 'distract' so global a gathering of prelates and pastors. The Cuban Missile Crisis began during its maiden week (providing much of the impetus for, and subtext of, Chenu's 'Message'). The Fathers' approving, 'almost triumphantly so' (Congar), the final version of *Sacrosanctum Concilium* made 22 November 1963 a real red-letter day in conciliar business. But any celebrations were eclipsed within hours, as news of John F. Kennedy's death began reaching Rome. Earlier that month, the assassination of another Catholic premier, South Vietnam's US-backed President Diệm, sparked widespread concern among the bishops. For one of them, Archbishop Thục of Huế, the geopolitical was also the personal: as the slain politician's elder brother, he would never return to his native Vietnam (Figure 5).

These examples could easily be multiplied. It is no surprise that a Council convened in the famously febrile 1960s should have felt a duty to speak out on the myriad topics undergirding 'the joys and the hopes, the griefs and the anxieties of the men of this age' (*Gaudium et Spes* 1). A few of these topics got a dedicated, if short, 'Declaration' or 'Decree' of their own—as was the case with religious liberty, the media (see below), and the Church's relationships with non-Christian religions. Most, however, simply got added to Schema XIII, which would ultimately become the above-quoted *Gaudium et Spes*. Its formal title is the Pastoral

New York City
Sept.12,1963

Viet-Namese Prelate Poses Delicate Problem for Pope

5. Archbishop Ngô Đình Thục of Huế, younger brother to South Vietnam's President Diệm.

Constitution on the Church in the World of Today (i.e. *Mundo Huius Temporis*, literally 'World of this Time'; the more common 'Modern World' obscures its speaking-to-the-present-moment intention and urgency). A footnote explains that 'Pastoral', as distinct from the other three 'Dogmatic' Constitutions, denotes the fact that, while it does contain a good deal of doctrine, much of the text is devoted to specific applications. Hence, 'Some elements have a permanent value; others, only a transitory one... Interpreters must bear in mind... the changeable circumstances which the subject matter, by its very nature, involves.' While novel in the context of an ecumenical council, this basic approach—'counsels of imperfection', in the waggish words of Edward Hadas—has been common in the periodic 'Social Teaching' encyclicals, beginning with Leo XIII's *Rerum Novarum* in 1891.

By their very nature, Vatican II's statements to and about the 'outside world' (albeit one which, as it is keen to stress, Christians themselves are an integral part of: 'truly linked with mankind and its history by the deepest of bonds' (GS 1)) have provided ample scope for disagreement. This was so among the Fathers themselves. After all, trying adequately to comment on such complex topics as, say, war and peace, marriage and family, poverty, economics, food security, population growth, nuclear proliferation, the relationship between science and religion, contemporary unbelief, race relations, political self-determination, and a great deal else *in a single document* was always going to be a big ask. The observation by Archbishop Hurley (Durban, South Africa) during the Fourth Session that 'in many cases the Fathers who discussed economics sounded like men out of their depth', no doubt applied more widely during the Schema XIII debates. Nowhere was their glaring lack of 'lived experience' more obvious than when discussing women or married life. Addressing the subcommission drafting what would ultimately become paragraphs 47–52, the Mexican auditor Luz María Álvarez-Icaza pointed out: 'Since I am the only married woman here, I feel I have the responsibility of saying that when we have had intercourse, giving life to our children, it wasn't an act of concupiscence but an act of love, and I believe this is true of most Christian mothers who conceived a child.' The relevant passage was duly changed.

Some bishops expressed frustration at a disproportionate focus on First World problems, especially in earlier drafts: 'The schema has been conceived for Europe and perhaps for America, but not sufficiently for the Third World', to quote Archbishop Tchidimbo of Conakry in Guinea. The frenetic pace of the Council's final months was, moreover, a far cry from the comparatively leisurely process of discussion and text-tweaking enjoyed by *Sacrosanctum Concilium* and *Lumen Gentium*. Of the Council's 16 documents, 11 were promulgated during the 12 weeks allotted to the Fourth Session. *Gaudium et Spes* was one of four greenlighted on 7 December 1965, the day before Paul VI formally closed Vatican II.

Schema thirteen is vast in its scope,
it bravely endeavours to cope
  with all the world's ills,
  plus anovulant pills:
to complete it we haven't a hope.

John O'Loughlin (1911–85), limerick composed during Council

Bishop of Darwin (Australia), 1949–85

De Huius Temporis Ecclesia decretum
omnia tractat apud Coetum:
  res magnas et pusillas,
  anovulantes pastillas;
quod videndi spes nulla expletum.

Bernard Wall (1894–1976), Latin translation of above

Bishop of Brentwood (England), 1955–69

While it would be fair to describe the document as uneven, this ought neither to detract nor distract from its genuine merits. In showing how the largely abstract teachings of other documents might be applied in the real world, *Gaudium et Spes*'s overarching vision is of abiding significance. After all, it is one thing to *say* that 'the laity consecrate the world itself to God' (*Lumen Gentium* 34). It's quite another to describe, even if in general terms, what that might *look* like in practice: 'Almost more important than the solutions offered by the text is the attitude behind the text…The Council had the courage to produce a public document that…sought to begin a task that would continue' (Ratzinger, writing in 1966). What's more, even at the level of specifics, *Gaudium et Spes* includes many genuine highpoints of the Council's teachings. We will consider one such case-study—on war and peace—later on in this chapter, though several more could have been chosen. First though, we shall explore two notable aspects of the Council's engagement with the wider world which

We live in a world, in which 200 million people would willingly take the vow of poverty tomorrow, if they could live as well, be clothed as well, and be housed as well as I am—or even some who take the vow of poverty.

The greater number of bishops in this Council are living in want or in persecution, and they come from all peoples and all nations.

As only a wounded Christ could convert a doubting Thomas, so only a Church wounded by poverty can convert a doubting world.

Fulton Sheen (1895–1979), Council speech, November 1964

Auxiliary bishop of New York, 1951–66; appointed bishop of Rochester in 1966

received their own documents: the media (*Inter Mirifica*) and Judaism (*Nostra Aetate*).

Media: 'among the wondrous things'

Ever since the calling of a Council made headlines across the globe—'MOVE CALLED "EPOCHAL"', cried the front page of the *New York Times*; 'ENDING THE SCHISMS?', asked the *Guardian*—the world's media had taken a keen interest in proceedings. While that was also true of Vatican I, its reporting was done by train and telegraph. A century later, a cornucopia of 'wonderful technological discoveries... which have uncovered new avenues of communicating most readily news, views and teachings of every sort' had become available to 'reach and influence, not only individuals, but the very masses and the whole of human society' (*Inter Mirifica* 1). Radio, television, and film were all very much a part of the conciliar event. This was most obviously so via reporting on, and indeed interpreting, the Council to the world outside. Even though excluded from the Aula itself, journalists found no shortage of willing informants, interviewees, or op-ed writers from among the participants. (In a December 1965 diary entry, Henri de Lubac remarks archly that some fellow *periti* 'have been present more often in the newsrooms than in the work meetings'.) These reports were consumed avidly by Catholics throughout the world, playing a major role in how Vatican II was received in real time. No doubt some diocesan bishops, returning home after months in Rome, soon found their perspective on 'What the Council Wants' to be at odds with the received wisdom among their own clergy and laity.

The media's influence was likewise felt within the Council, since the participants also read newspapers and listened to the radio. Indeed, many soon found that a well-placed interview was a better way to get 'heard' by their fellow bishops than a Latin speech on the Aula floor. The press also, of course, reported reactions to the Council's deliberations from diverse sources: editorials, opinion pieces, vox pops, petitions, statements from this or that interest group. Bishops were, naturally enough, keen to know the 'climate of public opinion' in their home countries and dioceses, and could hardly help but be influenced by it. Some Fathers found this feedback hugely beneficial: 'the way in which public opinion propagated the Council exceeded all forecasts', as Austria's Cardinal König later recalled. Others felt it created a distorting Hall of Mirrors. Lamenting the 'terrible power' of the media's 'new magisterium', France's Archbishop Lefebvre asked: 'How many Fathers have sought to be the mouthpiece of this "public opinion"? How many others have approved these interventions from fear of failing to conform to this new teaching?'

Given the importance of the media to understanding Vatican II and its reception, its own direct engagement with the topic may seem rather meagre. At a little over 2,000 words in Latin, the 'Decree on the Media of Social Communications' is among the Council's shortest, and is often considered (if it is considered at all) among its least impressive. While the original preparatory

Schema on the subject was one of the few to survive the general cull of the opening weeks, few Fathers ever really seemed to warm to it. Little time was allotted to its discussion—barely three mornings during the First Session—and while there were a couple of attempts to have it pulled from the agenda entirely, no one was willing to expend overmuch 'political capital' so early on to oppose it. In the event, it was ushered over the line in November 1963, in part because the Council's overseers wanted to have more than just the liturgy Constitution to show for two whole sessions of work.

The impression of many bishops that *Inter Mirifica* was unworthy of an ecumenical council was perhaps as much a comment on the subject matter as on the contents of the text itself. While papal encyclicals had addressed the topic in the past, there was undoubtedly a feeling that *councils* were supposed to deal with weighty matters of dogma. 'Media studies' was, therefore, felt to be beneath the dignity of a conciliar decree. And to be fair, *Inter Mirifica* is hardly ground-breaking in its theoretical approach. That modern technology can be both a blessing and a curse (§2), that news reporting should 'always be true and complete, within the bounds of justice and charity' (§5), or that young people should practise 'moderation and self-control' in media consumption and not believe everything they watch or read (§10)—none of these were original insights in the early 1960s. (Though to be fair, they're even less so now, yet that doesn't stop them being the cornerstones of 'media literacy' efforts.)

More intellectually promising is an emphasis on the need 'to take into consideration the entire situation or circumstances, namely, the persons, place, time, and other conditions under which communication takes place', and to be mindful of 'the precise manner in which a given medium achieves its effect' (§4). These hints at a more nuanced, socio-cultural approach to understanding the media were genuinely cutting-edge. The Canadian philosopher and media theorist Marshall McLuhan had published *The Gutenberg Galaxy*, in which such ideas take centre-stage, the year before *Inter Mirifica*'s promulgation; he would coin the phrase 'the medium is the message' the year after it. Given both that McLuhan was a committed Catholic, and that *Inter Mirifica* is insistent that the laity should bring their 'technical, economic, cultural and artistic talents' (§13) to the media sphere, there is a pleasing neatness about this.

The Jews: 'Most dear to God'

Viewed in hindsight, it's hard to imagine that an ecumenical council held so soon after the Shoah could not have felt it imperative to say something on the relationship between Christians and Jews. But it was by no means a foregone conclusion. The topic was only explicitly added to the Council's agenda in 1960, at the personal instigation of Pope John, following a private meeting between him and the French Jewish historian Jules Isaac (a leading figure in the growing world of Christian–Jewish friendship and dialogue after the war). The task of scoping out what this might look like was given to the German Jesuit Cardinal Augustin Bea's newly created Secretariat for Christian Unity. While that looks like a strange choice of home for such a topic, it testifies both to the lack of formal organs within the Curia for thinking about Christian–Jewish relations, and to the suitability of the biblical scholar Bea and his team. Notably, this included the *periti* John Oesterreicher (a pre-war convert from Judaism, whose parents were murdered at Theresienstadt and Auschwitz), and Gregory Baum (also a convert; born in Germany to a Jewish mother and Protestant father, he came to Canada in 1940 as a refugee), both of whom played important roles in drafting the final text. Bea also sought, and received, detailed advice from Jewish scholars, most notably the Polish-American rabbi Abraham Heschel.

It soon became apparent that Judaism was, so to speak, the Council's super-charged 'third rail'—any attempt to touch it might short-circuit, or else electrocute, other core aspects of its programme. Before the Council even began, rumours that it was planning to say something positive on the Jews sparked outcry in the Arab world, where such plans were viewed as a thinly veiled political affirmation of the State of Israel, established in 1948; the influential Cairo-based radio station *Sawt al-Arab* saw it all as a 'world Zionist plot to capitalize on the Vatican Council'. This in turn raised protests from representatives of various Eastern and Oriental Orthodox Churches, who were motivated both by political exigencies and by doctrinal concerns (among some of whom anything less than a forthright affirmation of the Jews' perpetual accursedness was tantamount to apostasy). Either way, it did not augur well for what was supposed to be a primary task of the Council, and moreover of Bea's own department: bridge-building with 'the separated brethren'. All of this generated deep misgivings on the part of the Middle Eastern bishops, not least due to very real fears of reprisals against their own already vulnerable flocks. Furthermore, most of these bishops came from the Eastern Catholic Churches—the Maronites, Melkites, Syriacs, Copts, and Chaldeans—and repairing past wrongs (not least, Latin high-handedness and general ignorance of, and lack of sympathy for, their particular circumstances) was itself emerging as an important goal of the conciliar agenda. There was also a small but active anti-Semitic contingent within the Council itself: a tome entitled *The Plot Against the Church* was mysteriously distributed to all the bishops during the First Session, and talk of 'Jewish freemasonry' was occasionally heard on the Council floor—most notably from Cardinal Ruffini (Palermo, Italy)—during later debates. For all these reasons, and indeed several more, plans to discuss a draft text 'on the Jews' during the First Session were quietly, and indefinitely, shelved.

This, however, placed the Council in a further bind. *Not* to address the issue, having raised hopes that it would, was not really an option either. The failure to speak out, and especially to denounce the many wrongs done (and still being done) in Christianity's name to the Jewish people, would—in very different quarters from those cited above—itself be unforgivable. The 'optics' of this became all the more apparent in 1963, with the release of the German author Rolf Hochhuth's still-controversial play *The Deputy*, impugning Pope Pius XII's conduct in the face of Nazi atrocities. In the face of the Vatican's efforts to deny the play's charge of 'guilt by silence' (as Hannah Arendt phrased it in her own review), the ongoing uncertainty over the Council's statement hardly helped. The controversy rumbled on throughout 1964 and into 1965, casting a shadow over Paul VI's historic pilgrimage to the Holy Land that January, with the pope feeling the need to decry the 'suspicions and even accusations…levelled against the memory of this great Pontiff'. The following month the banning of the play in Rome, at the Vatican's request, sparked not only a further wave of headlines, but even a terrorist attack: a bomb blast at the gates of Vatican City was thought to be the work of communist militants, protesting the censorship.

Over the course of the Second, Third, and Fourth Sessions, *De Iudaeis* was something of a shape-shifting, floating paragraph, tweaked multiple times to refine, remove, or restore this or that phrase (the insertion, and later withdrawal, of a direct disavowal of the explicit charge of 'deicide'—literally 'God-killing'—against the Jewish people being the most famous example) and slated for inclusion in several different texts at various times. Too short to be a declaration or decree in its own right, it was finally decided to incorporate it into a more wide-ranging statement on the non-Christian religions.

This was largely a tactical manoeuvre—a means of taking the focus off Judaism alone, and to be able to balance it with positive comments on Buddhism, Hinduism, and Islam too. In truth, dedicated statements on these religions were no bad things in themselves: after all, if atheists could be so honoured (i.e. *Gaudium et Spes* 19–21, regarded by Ratzinger as 'among the most important pronouncements of Vatican II'), then why not the

We must deny that the Jews are guilty of the death of our Saviour except insofar as all men have sinned and on that account crucified him and, indeed, still crucify him...

All of us have seen the evil fruit of this kind of false reasoning. In this august assembly, in this solemn moment, we must cry out: There is no Christian rationale—neither theological nor historical—for any inequity, hatred or persecution of our Jewish brothers...

In this our age, how many have suffered! How many have died because of the indifference of Christians, because of silence! There is no need to enumerate the crimes committed in our own time. If not many Christian voices were lifted in recent years against the great injustices, yet let our voices humbly cry out now.

Richard Cushing (1895–1970), Council speech, September 1964

Archbishop of Boston, 1944–70; appointed cardinal in 1958

members of other religions too? It is true that *Lumen Gentium* (on salvation) and *Ad Gentes* (on the missions) also touched on these topics, but nowhere in the conciliar corpus was there an attempt to offer an overarching 'theology of the religions'. Furthermore, given that millions of Catholics throughout the world lived and worked alongside Hindus, Muslims, and Buddhists (and adherents of numerous other faiths), it would have been strange not to have something to say about how Christians ought to relate to them. Some Council Fathers would have liked to see even more; Archbishop Thục, for instance, considered it 'scandalous' that there were no invited interfaith observers alongside the ecumenical ones. On strictly theological grounds, given the *sui generis* relationship of Christianity to Judaism—'the bond that spiritually ties the people of the New Covenant to Abraham's stock' (*Nostra Aetate* 4)—it is undeniably awkward for Judaism to be subsumed into a wider and more general 'world religions' framework. However, as is clear from the above, there were more than strictly theological considerations in play.

A good portion of the final statement affirms, with gratitude, 'the spiritual patrimony common to Christians and Jews', and encourages Christians to learn more about it. Critically, this deep connection is not conceived purely as a thing of the past. Commenting on the text in 1970, the *peritus* John Oesterreicher highlighted especially its use of present verbs: 'Even though it is not spelled out in the text that Judaism is a living force, it is implicit in these recommendations of the Council. It is not to the Israel of old that the church extends her brotherly—or if you prefer her sisterly—hand, but to the Jews here and now.' In large part, however, this is made possible by what *Nostra Aetate* does say about the past: 'True, the Jewish authorities and those who followed their lead pressed for the death of Christ; still, what happened in His passion cannot be charged against all the Jews, without distinction, then alive, nor against the Jews of today. Although the Church is the new people of God, the Jews should not be presented as rejected or accursed by God, as if this followed from the Holy Scriptures' (NA 4). This passage has often been glossed as Vatican II 'absolving' the Jewish people from collective guilt over the death of Christ. But this is not so. Rather, it is a denial that Jews-in-general, either then or thereafter, ever shared in any collective guilt in the first place—over and above, that is, the collective guilt of *all* human beings, very much including Christians (a point that, as was noted during the Aula debates, the *Catechism of the Council of Trent* made in the 16th century).

Having issued this clarification, the Council proceeds—finally—to state unequivocally that: 'the Church, mindful of the patrimony she shares with the Jews and moved not by political reasons but by the Gospel's spiritual love, decries hatred, persecutions, [and] displays of anti-Semitism, directed against Jews at any time and by anyone'. For the Catholic Church to issue such a statement shouldn't have proven so controversial. But it was.

War: 'never again'

Coming in the wake of two devastating world wars, and with the Cold War superpowers poised on the brink of mutual annihilation, Vatican II was never going to be hawkishly militarist. Blessing the peacemakers had, moreover, been a distinctive emphasis of recent popes, if to little evident avail. Benedict XV's 1914 jeremiad at the start of the First World War—'On every side the dread phantom of war holds sway... The combatants are the greatest and wealthiest nations of the earth; what wonder, then, if, well provided with the most awful weapons modern military science has devised, they strive to destroy one another with refinements of horror' (*Ad Beatissimi Apostolorum* 3)—could have been issued almost unchanged 50 years later. John XXIII's encyclical *Pacem in Terris*, promulgated just seven weeks before his death in June 1963, added a valedictory 'steer' to the Council's agenda on these matters. So too did Pope Paul VI's overnight trip to New York (itself a remarkable illustration of what *Gaudium et Spes* would term 'a new stage of history') in October 1964, to tell the United Nations: 'the blood of millions, countless unheard-of sufferings, useless massacres and frightening ruins have sanctioned the agreement that unites you with an oath that ought to change the future history of the world: never again war, never again war! It is peace, peace, that has to guide the destiny of the nations of all mankind!' Coming just days before he opened the Third Session, during which Schema XIII's draft paragraphs on war and peace were due to be discussed, the 'Papal will'—something which, on other topics, could often seem more like a 'Papal will-o'-the-wisp' to those delegates eager to second-guess it—was unambiguous.

The real debates were, therefore, over the details. The issue of just *how* comprehensive, *how* unqualified, *how* (un)admitting-of-legitimate-exceptions was a source of major disagreements. The maximalists were certainly well represented. Cardinal Ottaviani (Figure 6), for example, had long been famous for his irenicism: his 1947 textbook, no doubt familiar to many bishops who had studied in Rome, argued that 'no conceivable cause could ever be sufficient justification for the evils, the slaughter, the destruction, the moral and religious upheavals which war today entails'. On the Council floor, he went even further, demanding that not only war, but also 'those things which have some kind of kinship with war'—that is, espionage, sabotage, stirring up revolutions, aiding guerrillas—be unequivocally condemned. He also called for 'the creation of one world republic... in which no longer would there be strife among various nations, but an entire world living in peace'.

While Ottaviani may have been at a slight extreme, he was—for once—not far out of step with the growing consensus. This real prospect of a blanket condemnation of all wars, plus much else in the modern 'all measures short of war' playbook, in turn provoked a rearguard action, focused on securing a select number of important qualifications. Bishop Hannan, an auxiliary of Washington, DC (though he would end the Council as Archbishop of New Orleans), voiced fears that the draft text 'seems to ignore the common teaching of the Church and the norms to be applied in the conduct of a just war'. Though stressing that 'we hold war in horror', he stressed the moral permissibility, perhaps even necessity, of fighting in the cause of defence or liberation. He also urged the Council to record 'a word of praise in favour of those who defend liberty as well as those who freely offered their lives so that we may enjoy the freedom of the sons of God'. Having served as a paratrooper chaplain during the Allied invasion of Europe, including the liberation of the Wöbbelin concentration camp, these were topics close to his own heart. The Council ultimately accepted the force of this minority report, with *Gaudium et Spes* admitting that 'governments cannot be denied the right to legitimate defense once every means of peaceful settlement has been exhausted', and that those 'who devote themselves to the

6. Cardinal Alfredo Ottaviani (left), with Pope Paul VI.

military service of their country should regard themselves as the agents of security and freedom of peoples. As long as they fulfill this role properly, they are making a genuine contribution to the establishment of peace' (GS 79).

Alongside its overall teaching on 'the fostering of peace', which it is careful to stress is not merely limited to 'the absence of war' (GS 78), *Gaudium et Spes* devotes special attention to 'scientific weapons' (GS 80). The phrasing is certainly awkward, but the intention seems to be a catch-all term for the atomic, biological, and chemical weapons which several influential Fathers, such as Patriarch Maximos IV of Antioch, demanded the Council condemn outright. Others urged a degree of circumspection, at least as regards atomic weapons. Liverpool's Archbishop Beck suggested that the Council couldn't definitively rule out the possibility of a defensive (and morally defensible) use of 'nuclear weapons even of vast force', citing the example of a pre-emptive strike against a bomb-bearing satellite. Another English bishop, Leeds's George Dwyer, also mooted the feasibility of very small, precisely targeted nuclear weapons as a plausibly 'just' deployment. While not alone in floating such hypotheticals, it was surely telling that the (howsoever qualified) defenders of nuclear weapons all seemed to hail from countries—Britain, France, the USA—that already had them. On slightly firmer conciliar ground, therefore, were those framing the permissibility of nuclear weapons in terms of possession, rather than putative uses. Thus Beck also urged that in 'certain circumstances peace can be assured only by what has been called "the balance of terror"', and advised the Council against condemning 'those governments . . . which have succeeded in keeping peace however tentative in the world' by means of such deterrence. Accordingly, the final text strikes an uneasy balance between a forthright statement of principle and grudging concession to life in a fallen world. Regarding the former, for example, 'Any act of war aimed indiscriminately at the destruction of entire cities . . . is a crime against God and man himself . . . and merits unequivocal and unhesitating condemnation' (GS 80). (Note that the Latin wording here is even stronger than the English suggests: *damnandum est* literally means 'is to be cursed/damned'. This has a very similar semantic range to the classic *anathema sit*, while technically still allowing the Council to maintain that it 'pronounced no anathemas'.) In stark contrast, while the *fact* of nuclear deterrence is acknowledged ('this accumulation of arms, which increases each year, likewise serves . . . as deterrent to possible enemy attack'), no direct comment is made as to whether engaging in it is licit or not. The most the text will say is that 'Many regard this procedure as the most effective way by which peace of a sort can be maintained between nations at the present time.' Irrespective of whether these unnamed 'many' are correct or not, it is nevertheless the case that 'the arms race is an utterly treacherous trap for humanity' (GS 81).

True, such wrangled-over 'compromise statements'—and this is by no means the only such example in the conciliar corpus—often end up satisfying no one. And indeed the phrase 'composition by committee', often invoked in discussions of magisterial documents, is rarely meant as a compliment. But one might equally argue that this method can—and in this case, certainly did—result in finely nuanced treatments of deeply complex topics. And that, furthermore, the need to take the 'minority view' into account in the final text ensured the inclusion of important principles and perspectives that would otherwise have been eclipsed.

This point certainly applies elsewhere in the Council documents too. But it is particularly clear here, given just how much 'politicking' surrounded these few paragraphs of Schema XIII both within and without the Council itself. International Catholic peace groups lobbied hard, working in close concert with a network of influential bishops. These included Cardinals Suenens (Mechelen-Brussels, Belgium), König (Vienna, Austria), Alfrink (Utrecht, Netherlands), and Ritter (St Louis, USA), as well as Archbishop Roberts of Bombay, India. Lay activists also ensured that their views were heard, including on the Council floor itself via official 'auditor' interventions (though these groups' attempts to have female *auditrices* address the Fathers were officially denied as being 'premature'). A 10-day fast for peace by 20 Catholic women, undertaken in Rome at the beginning of the Fourth Session, also attracted much attention. Incidentally, it also meant that one of the fasters, the American pacifist Dorothy Day, co-founder of the Catholic Worker Movement, had a captive audience of 35 bishops on the voyage over. One suspects that she did not waste her opportunity. No doubt a good deal of lobbying, much of it out of the public eye, also went into making sure that the 'other side' was heard too. An open letter written by Catholic members of the CIA and other US agencies, albeit 'writing in a personal capacity', was probably not the only overture coming from those quarters, given the geopolitical situation. Politicking at ecumenical councils is nothing new, however: had we the profusion of notes, drafts, interviews, media reports, diaries, and reminiscences for Nicaea or Chalcedon that we have for Vatican II, we'd see just how true that is.

Chapter 8
Conciliar 'hermeneutics': making sense of the debates over Vatican II

Vatican II ushered in an era of dynamism, excitement, and upheaval. At least for modern Catholicism, the rapidity of change in the Church in the first decade after the Council was unprecedented. These, on top of all the other 'profound and rapid changes spreading by degrees around the whole world' (*Gaudium et Spes* 4) from the 1960s onwards, lent something of a runaway, rollercoaster feel to the immediate postconciliar period. Rollercoasters exhilarate and energize some people. Others feel sick and want to get off (Figure 7).

Moreover, the changes themselves did not always, obviously, or everywhere produce positive results. Aspects of this were noted in Chapter 4, with regard to the Church's liturgical life. But very similar stories, with analogously plummeting statistics, can be told regarding several indicators of pastoral health. In many countries, the sometimes-radical 'renewals' of priestly and religious life coincided with large numbers leaving their vows and vocations, and steep declines in those willing to replace them. In some nations, Catholic universities and schools—which received their own conciliar Declaration (*Gravissimum Educationis*)—began noticeably to secularize. Repeated surveys of European and North American laity, who 'dedicated to Christ and anointed by the Holy Spirit, are marvellously called and wonderfully prepared so that ever more abundant fruits of the Spirit may be produced in them'

(*Lumen Gentium* 34), found progressively lower levels of Catholic practice, belief, or moral attitudes among them with each passing year. Most damningly of all, whatever alleged benefits the Council's attentions brought to seminary formation, church governance, the theology of the episcopacy, or canon law, none of them prevented the vast numbers of horrifying instances of sexual abuse and cover-up that have come to light in recent decades.

Our point here is not (necessarily) to blame the Council, directly or indirectly, for any of these outcomes. Just as Vatican II did not occur in a vacuum, its subsequent interpretation and implementation did not play out in one. 'Post hoc' does not, moreover, logically entail 'propter hoc'. Perhaps some of the above would have been even worse had there been no Council—or if it had played out, and/or been received and implemented, very differently. Then again, perhaps some would have been much

"Your disguises are excellent, gentlemen—but, as reverend mother here points out, somewhat outdated!"

7. Cartoon by John Ryan, published in *The Catholic Herald*, Late 1960s or early 1970s.

better had there been no Council at all. Our point, rather, is that given all this, it should not be surprising that there has emerged a great deal of discussion and debate, some of it acrimonious, about Vatican II and its legacy. And indeed, it is striking just how quickly even some of the Council's most active contributors were expressing quite serious misgivings about, if not the Council itself, then the various ways in which it was being read and received. Most notably, Paul VI observed in a 1972 homily that 'it was believed that after the Council would come a day of sunshine in the history of the Church. Instead there has come a day of clouds, storms, darkness, searching, uncertainty.' He famously ascribed this mismatch to the fact that 'from some fissure the smoke of Satan has entered the temple of God'. Those of a less apocalyptic mindset might substitute what the sociologist Robert K. Merton called the law of 'unanticipated consequences of social action'.

This process of the *reception* of Vatican II—that is, how the Council was understood and implemented, challenged or celebrated, debated or rejected—is a process that continues to this day. One important way to chronicle the reception of Vatican II is to examine the different *hermeneutical* approaches to the Council: that is, the basic interpretative lenses through which Catholics (and others) understand Vatican II, its teaching, and its significance. Thus, we present here four very general hermeneutical paradigms through which Catholics have understood Vatican II in the last 50-odd years.

Just like the conciliar event itself, paradigms for interpreting it cannot exist in a vacuum either. That is, postconciliar paradigms react to and are shaped by the most pivotal events and personalities connected to the reception of Vatican II, from the (in)famous birth control encyclical *Humanae Vitae* in 1968 to the larger-than-life personality and influence of John Paul II (pope from 1978 to 2005) to contemporary calls for 'synodality'. What follows certainly privileges academic and ecclesial interpreters of the Council and the debates they have engaged in over the last

> The pontificate of John XXIII, and then the Council, seemed to have inaugurated an unhoped for (if not undreamt of!) renewal in the Catholic Church. It is true that there had been a gradual rediscovery of the Bible and the Church Fathers; there was also the liturgical movement, ecumenism, and . . . a rediscovery of the Church herself in her most authentic tradition, combined with a determined opening out to the scientific, cultural and social problems of the world . . . Suddenly, or at least rapidly, the whole movement began to win over the body of the Church through its having been imposed on her leaders. Only a few years have gone by since then, but, we must admit, what has followed so far does not seem to have produced much of a response to one's expectation. Unless we are blind, we must even state bluntly that what we see looks less like the hoped-for regeneration of Catholicism than its accelerated decomposition.
>
> **Louis Bouyer (1913–2004)**; writing in 1968
>
> French *peritus* and member of liturgy commission

half-century. This is by no means the only way to tell the story of Vatican II's reception and interpretation. For example, there is a great deal of sociological research on the impact of the Council on normal Catholics (and on non-Catholics) in the pew: men and women, lay and clerical, rich and poor, Western and non-Western. Nevertheless, the hermeneutical paradigms held by Catholic clergy (especially popes) and academics, and the debates they engage in, are pivotal lenses through which the Council has been and continues to be interpreted. Such interpretations affect the life of the Catholic Church in profound ways. While some of these discussions might seem highly technical, the purview only of those few with the leisure and training to read lengthy books in multiple languages, these hermeneutical battles flow from lecture halls and sacristies in Rome and South Bend and Manila to seminaries, parishes, and Catholic classrooms around the world.

If you look at the history of the Church, you find that every great Council has been followed by a crisis. There are always some people who hang on to the past and make it their duty to defend the true Church. They exaggerate. And there are always others who exaggerate in the opposite direction. Balance is something that men find very difficult . . .

Attitudes and structures were so profoundly shaken by the Council that it would have been inconceivable for everything to go smoothly, quietly and harmoniously afterwards. It would have been disturbing if there hadn't been collisions and clashes and conflicts: it would have meant that the Council had said and done nothing.

Hélder Câmara (1909–1999); interview in 1977

Auxiliary bishop of Rio de Janeiro (Brazil), 1952–64; Archbishop of Olinda e Recife, 1964–85

They profoundly shape the Church's interaction with the modern cultural and political order, with other Christians, and with non-Christians.

Four major positions on Vatican II

Our four paradigms are, in brief: (1) the Traditionalist Paradigm: suspicion or rejection of the Council; (2) the Failure Paradigm: progressive suspicion or rejection of Vatican II as an unsuccessful reform attempt; (3) the Spirit-Event Paradigm: acceptance or celebration of the Council, but with a prioritization of the spirit of Vatican II, an insistence on doctrinal change and innovation, and an understanding of the Council as primarily an 'event'; (4) the Text-Continuity Paradigm: acceptance or celebration of Vatican II, but with a prioritization of the final texts, an emphasis on doctrinal continuity, and an understanding of the Council as primarily the promulgation of a body of teaching. These precise groupings are our own, but draw on the insights of Gavin D'Costa,

Peter Steinfels, Massimo Faggioli, and others. One of us went into more detail about these four paradigms in a previous book with the same publisher.

The Traditionalist Paradigm: conservative suspicion or rejection of the Council

This paradigm can be summed up through the following assertion: the Council erred or was dangerously ambiguous; it did too much and changed too much. As we saw, a small but vocal minority at the Council itself publicly conveyed their deep misgivings about the general orientation of Vatican II and some of the conciliar texts (e.g. *Dignitatis Humanae*). Catholics of this mindset virtually unanimously accepted the Council, and simply tried to mitigate the perceived damage. Only very small groups of critics formally refused to accept Vatican II. The most famous—or infamous—point of resistance coalesced as the Society of St Pius X (SSPX), under the leadership of Marcel Lefebvre, the French archbishop who had been an outspoken member of the conciliar Minority (see Chapter 3).

The Traditionalist Paradigm, as we conceive it, is about phenomena much broader and more diffuse than ecclesial organizations like SSPX, who formally reject the Council. Catholics who are suspicious of Vatican II or who wish to marginalize or 'leave it behind' broadly fit into our first paradigm. These interpreters might be academically marginal in most cases, but they are a significant force in some sectors of the clergy, especially in the United States and parts of Europe (France, England, etc.). The great majority of Traditionalist Paradigm Catholics are in full communion with the Church and are often attached to various traditionalist religious orders and educational institutions; they are not formally schismatic or in an 'irregular' situation like the SSPX. Postconciliar 'Traditionalism' as a discernible and self-conscious movement remains very small. Nevertheless the *de iure*, or, more often, de facto rejection of the Council or at least of its implementation remains a serious issue for contemporary Catholicism. The postconciliar popes have tried to accommodate and dialogue with schismatic and non-schismatic Traditionalist Paradigm interpreters in different, and sometimes seemingly incompatible, ways.

The Failure Paradigm: progressive suspicion or rejection of the Council

The Failure Paradigm has very different concerns from the Traditionalist Paradigm, but both perspectives generally agree that the Council, while perhaps containing a great deal of positive elements, is ultimately not the lodestar for the contemporary Church that mainstream Catholicism sets it up as. Failure Paradigm interpreters come in two main types; they can be termed 'methodological' and 'doctrinal' critics. The prominent voices in this paradigm are often academics or lower clergy—and almost never high-ranking prelates, since, among other reasons, the postconciliar popes and the episcopal hierarchies they have shaped are typically hostile to this paradigm.

'Methodological' critics believe that the Council never had a chance for relevance because there was something defective in the theological methodology of the Council Fathers—that is, in the specific ways they did theology and understood the Church and the problems facing it, perhaps even the basic way they saw the world. Critics who see Vatican II as 'too late and irrelevant' (to quote D'Costa's description) often come from liberationist, feminist, or postmodernist perspectives.

The second kind of Failure Paradigm interpreters, 'doctrinal' critics, straddle the boundary of the Spirit-Event Paradigm (described below). They typically laud John XXIII and his call for *aggiornamento*; the *ressourcement* movements are seen as, at least, good starts. But, they believe the positive conciliar spirit was betrayed at some point. For many this betrayal actually began during the Council itself, for example through Paul VI's excessive concessions to the Minority, which rendered certain key texts seriously defective. For others, this alleged betrayal is primarily about postconciliar back-tracking (most would cite both). Failure Paradigm critics praise elements of Vatican II reform, but these Catholics tend to locate serious, even crippling problems in *the texts themselves*, rather than just in their interpretation or in the postconciliar magisterium.

Postconciliar popes usually bear a good deal of blame in this narrative, especially John Paul II and Benedict XVI. For example, the liberation theologian José Comblin called the 1985 Extraordinary Synod convened by John Paul II an attempted 'reversal' of Vatican II, due to its emphasis on continuity and centralized authority. On the other hand, Catholics sceptical of progressive interpretations of Vatican II promoted the narrative of the 1985 *Ratzinger Report*, a long-form interview which castigated hermeneutics of 'discontinuity'. Some Failure Paradigm Catholics see in the election of Pope Francis a return to the initial dynamism of John XXIII, but others would point to his repeated affirmations of traditional teaching on, for example, gender and sexuality, and conclude that Francis, despite laudable statements and actions, is ultimately fool's gold for the progressive Catholic cause.

The Spirit-Event Paradigm: the Council as event

Mainstream Catholic theology tends to celebrate Vatican II rather than just accepting it. The paradigm which was predominant in academic Catholic discourse and in many ecclesial sectors after the Council (though it never enjoyed a total monopoly) we call the Spirit-Event Paradigm. Spirit-Event interpreters celebrate the Council. While by no means ignoring the text, they prioritize the 'spirit' of Vatican II, insist that positive doctrinal change and innovation occurred (a form of 'discontinuity'), and understand the Council as first and foremost an ecclesial 'event' rather than a collection of texts. A major criticism that Spirit-Event interpreters level is that those who so emphasize Vatican II's continuities are unable to positively account for its manifest discontinuities. An implicit theological claim within many Spirit-Event narratives is the belief that Pope John XXIII (and the Holy Spirit, prompting him) started the Church on a new or renewed path, a journey that has not yet been completed.

The structure of the most influential books written by Spirit-Event interpreters sheds light on their approach. The massive *History of Vatican II* project led by Giuseppe Alberigo (leader of the so-called 'Bologna school') is a chronological historical account that emphasizes the struggle for change. John O'Malley's *What Happened at Vatican II* (2008), probably the most important single overview of the Council written in English, is also a chronological historical account. It pays attention to the documents but is structured around the conciliar event itself, not the final texts. In intra-Catholic debate, this position does not attack the Vatican II documents as such, though compromises in the final texts and the interventions of Paul VI are pointed out and at times bemoaned. Postconciliar disappointments are also sometimes highlighted, for example the victory of tradition and continuity over innovation (and *aggiornamento*?) in Paul VI's 1968 promulgation of the 'birth control encyclical' *Humanae Vitae*, or in John Paul II's decidedly more authoritarian approach to theological dissent and his appointment, generally, of doctrinally 'loyal' bishops. For the many Catholic women, especially women religious, who experienced Vatican II and its immediate aftermath as an event of unprecedented openness, doctrinal rulings such as John Paul II's *Ordinatio Sacerdotalis* (1994), which came down decisively against women's ordination, felt like clericalist and patriarchal betrayals of the Council's spirit and the general direction the Church seemed to be headed in. Spirit-Event interpreters dismayed by such rulings would not make the jump to repudiate papal infallibility, though they clearly share some of the concerns of those in the Failure Paradigm. Rather, they would argue that John Paul's judgement was not infallible, thus hinting or stating outright that it could eventually be reconsidered or reversed (as also, they hope, could *Humanae Vitae*).

The Text-Continuity Paradigm: the Council as a body of teaching

Our final paradigm, 'Text-Continuity', is also a very common way to interpret the Council. It is rooted in ancient Catholic commitments to doctrinal clarity, stability, and continuity across the ages. But, more immediately, it is a direct reaction to postconciliar interpretations and practices that troubled many Catholics, including a great many who generally saw the Council positively and do not fit in our Traditionalist Paradigm. This Text-Continuity Paradigm was sanctioned by a number of senior prelates like Ratzinger/Benedict XVI, and, less consistently, by John Paul II. It argues for a hermeneutic of the Council that stresses 'continuity' with past teaching and avoids claiming the Council occasioned doctrinal 'rupture' and 'discontinuity'. In addition to Ratzinger, some important interpreters who hold this perspective from the English-speaking world are Cardinal Avery Dulles SJ, Matthew Levering, and D'Costa. On our definition, Text-Continuity interpreters accept or even celebrate the Council, prioritize the 16 final texts, emphasize doctrinal continuity, and understand the Council primarily as the promulgation of a body of teaching.

A hermeneutic of reform: continuity and discontinuity on different levels

One could boil down our four positions to the following assertions. (1) The Traditionalist Paradigm: Vatican II erred or was dangerously ambiguous; it did too much. (2) The Failure Paradigm: the Council did not go far enough or was blind to basic problems facing the Church. (3) The Spirit-Event Paradigm: the texts, but especially the new attitudes and orientations associated with the Council, can help the Church positively transition out of a defensive mentality to dialogue with and evangelize the modern world. (4) The Text-Continuity Paradigm: Vatican II's texts (rightly interpreted) are good and true documents, but much that is associated with the 'spirit of Vatican II' is wrong, unhelpful, or confusing. Most Catholic interpreters, including the vast majority of ecclesial leaders, basically approve of the Council and its texts (i.e. they are Text-Continuity or Spirit-Event interpreters).

It is important to point out that no sophisticated interpreter aware of the issues really advocates complete continuity or discontinuity with past Catholic tradition and doctrinal texts. In that sense, the hermeneutical debates between our positions three and four are really over *in what sense* the Council is continuous and discontinuous with prior teachings, attitudes, and practices. This clash of mainstream interpretative schools—what we call Spirit-Event and Text-Continuity paradigms—has been described many ways: conservatives vs liberals, *Communio* vs *Concilium* (two influential journals founded by opposing groups of *periti*), neo-Augustinian vs neo-Thomist, and *ressourcement* vs *aggiornamento*. Of course, none of these pairs are always mutually exclusive or necessarily oppositional, but the pairings do touch on important differences.

Though tensions certainly remain over the reception of Vatican II, there is actually a good deal of consensus on important matters between the Spirit-Event and Text-Continuity paradigms. Cardinal Ratzinger was elected Pope Benedict XVI in April 2005. That Christmas, the former Council *peritus* addressed the College of Cardinals, clarifying and deepening his highly publicized (and misunderstood) views on Vatican II, continuity, discontinuity, and the nature of reform. Benedict did not insist on a rigid and static 'hermeneutic of continuity' in which, for example, one should try to verbally square *Dignitatis Humanae* with the numerous encyclicals of the 18th and 19th centuries that clearly and unequivocally condemned religious liberty. Instead of such hermeneutical gymnastics, Ratzinger proposed a 'hermeneutic of reform' which encompasses 'continuity and discontinuity' but 'on different levels'. *Dignitatis Humanae*, not to mention a slew of postconciliar teaching, is clearly, manifestly, and obviously

> It is precisely in this combination of continuity and discontinuity at different levels that the very nature of true reform consists... The Second Vatican Council, recognizing and making its own an essential principle of the modern State with the Decree on Religious Freedom, has recovered the deepest patrimony of the Church. By so doing she can be conscious of being in full harmony with the teaching of Jesus himself (cf. Mt 22:21), as well as with the Church of the martyrs of all time.
>
> **Pope Benedict XVI** (Joseph Ratzinger), Christmas Address to the Roman Curia, 22 December 2005

discontinuous with some past teaching documents on some questions. And yet, the pope argued, the new Catholic understanding of religious liberty *is* continuous with a deeper tradition: that of the early Church and the example and witness of Jesus Christ. Such insights rely upon robust and dynamic understandings of development of doctrine and *ressourcement*—understandings which include the possibility of real change—as well as *Dei Verbum*'s Christocentric view of revelation and more scriptural approach to theology.

Pope Benedict merely sketched the broad contours of a 'hermeneutic of reform' in his 2005 Christmas address. Catholic theologians, however, are by and large no longer interested in the exhausted and stale narrative alternatives of static continuity or revolutionary discontinuity. Neither holds up historically or theologically, especially given renewed understandings of ecclesiology. A hermeneutic of reform (rather than 'continuity' or 'discontinuity') opens up paths that are Christocentric, theologically rich, and historically conscious. The only perspective that can unite the two mainstream interpretative paradigms is one that sees Vatican II as consisting of 'continuity and discontinuity on different levels'. John O'Malley picked up this concept of a 'hermeneutic of reform' as a potential way out of the impasses the debate over conciliar hermeneutics has faced. It is thus promising for postconciliar Catholic theology that O'Malley and Ratzinger—who are seen to occupy conflicting paradigms of conciliar interpretation—both celebrate a hermeneutical key of 'reform' that sidesteps an unhelpful binary to argue for 'continuity and discontinuity on different levels'.

The first post-Vatican II pope: Francis and a new stage of conciliar reception

Pope Francis, elected in March 2013 after the shocking resignation of Benedict XVI, is in a certain sense the first truly postconciliar pope. While Paul VI guided the first stage of the global reception of Vatican II, he was, of course, a conciliar pope in a very literal sense—he presided over three of the four sessions. John Paul II (1978–2005) and Benedict XVI (2005–13) were both intimately engaged in the conciliar proceedings, and their subsequent elections (as well as Ratzinger's role as John Paul II's righthand man at the Congregation for the Doctrine of the Faith) meant that for roughly 35 years these two men profoundly shaped the global reception of Vatican II.

Jorge Mario Bergoglio (b. 1936) was not even a priest when the Council concluded. When he became Father Bergoglio in 1969, Vatican II was a done deal and the liturgical and other reforms were being rolled out. While very much a man of the Council in the sense that he embodies and advances many popular currents of conciliar interpretation, Pope Francis rarely engages in the kind of debates that were so crucial (indeed, personal) for John Paul II and Benedict. Vatican II is simply a reality for Pope Francis, and rejecting it or seeking to roll it back is, for him, akin to an ecclesial case of King Canute forbidding the incoming tide to advance any further. For Francis, the Catholic Church he knows and ministers in simply *is* the Church of Vatican II—it is Catholicism as he has known it for the majority of his life and for all of his priestly ministry as a Jesuit, bishop, and then pope. This situation has not in itself caused a new stage in the global reception of Vatican II, but it helpfully illustrates the reality that we have entered one. Rather fittingly, this new stage of reception was portended by two monumental events: the first papal resignation since 1415 (or since 1294 if one defines 'resignation' as a voluntary act) and the election of the first non-European pope in over a millennium, the first ever pope from the so-called 'New World', and the first pope from the ranks of the greatest globe-trotting missionary order, the Jesuits.

Francis's relationship to the texts and event of Vatican II gives us an important window into his theological and socio-political priorities. The issues at stake in the ongoing Vatican dialogue with (sometimes it is a polemic at and about) traditionalists seem to be simply taken as read by Francis. He puts little energy into defending at the doctrinal level (or even explaining) modern Catholic commitments to religious freedom, liberal democracy, ecumenism, or interreligious dialogue. For Francis, these values are simply Catholic, and he has little interest in narrating or justifying the kind of 'before and after' one sees in interventions like Benedict XVI's 2005 Christmas address. The Argentinian pope also seems positively hostile to the kind of liturgical restorationism that regained a good deal of lost ground during Benedict's pontificate, greatly aided by the symbiotic vision Ratzinger had for the 'Extraordinary' (preconciliar) and 'Ordinary' (postconciliar) forms of the Roman Rite Mass articulated in *Summorum Pontificum* (2007). For example, in a 24 August 2017 address, Francis spoke of the Vatican II liturgical reforms as 'irreversible' judgements of 'the magisterium' of the Church.

Another interesting (albeit ominous) feature of the Francis pontificate is that the kind of fragile truce under John Paul II and Benedict XVI—in which it was taboo to openly attack Vatican II—is breaking down in certain quarters. Rhetoric attacking not just the interpretation or implementation of Vatican II, but the text itself, used to come primarily from schismatic voices with little to no audience. Such rhetoric has become much more widely diffused, especially in the English-speaking world. In the wake of something of a failed coup against Pope Francis, Archbishop Viganò, former nuncio to the United States, openly rejected Vatican II, comparing it to the Jansenist Synod of Pistoia and pinning much of the ills of the Church on the errors of the Council. Viganò received an unprecedented boost in publicity during Donald Trump's 2020 campaign, when the US President publicly commended the rogue bishop on social media for his support (Viganò released a statement christening Trump as a key leader of the 'children of light' set against the forces of the 'Deep State' and the 'Deep Church'). While Viganò is a renegade figure and an extreme case, explicitly anti-Vatican II views have quite clearly received a new lease of life in the increasingly polarized theological and political situation in countries like the United States.

In an effort to eventually extinguish these flames—though perhaps pouring kerosene on them, at least for the short term—Pope Francis issued a '*motu proprio*' called *Traditionis Custodes* in July 2021. This ecclesiastical legislation, akin to a papal executive order, effectively reversed Benedict XVI's broad permittance of the preconciliar Latin Mass. *Traditionis Custodes* is a fascinating papal offensive in the hermeneutical wars over Vatican II. It is the latest in a centuries-long series of Roman assertions of interpretative authority over the legacy of ecumenical councils.

In seeking to defend the legacy of the Council, Pope Francis is also, rather explicitly, defending the postconciliar papacy in general, which has tied its own authority ever more tightly and irrevocably to Vatican II. This is one of the most important developments in modern Catholicism, and a fact not without irony given the long history of tension between pope and council. The 'canonizations' (formal declarations of sainthood) of the pope who called the council (John XXIII), who led much of it and its initial implementation (Paul VI), and who celebrated and defended it throughout his long pontificate (John Paul II) can be read as part of a strategy and agenda that the modern papacy has deeply internalized. Whatever else it is, we should see *Traditionis Custodes* as a decisive contribution by Francis to the continued debate not just over Vatican II specifically, but over a broader postconciliar Catholic debate regarding the nature of doctrinal development—a process the papacy wishes to direct and control.

While there is more continuity between Pope Francis's socio-political and economic vision and that of his recent predecessors than is often recognized, there is no doubt that Francis's style, at least, is in certain ways radically new. Theologically and pastorally, he has clear affinities with the more moderate forms of Liberation Theology. In this sense as well, the Catholic Church has moved into a new phase of the reception of Vatican II: the chief players at the Council are almost all dead, and Catholicism's weight and vitality—from sheer numbers and birth rates, to religious vocations, to freshness of thought—continues to shift evermore to the global South. A typical Catholic today is a young Brazilian, Nigerian, or Filipino, not an elderly Italian or Bavarian. While Vatican II was the first ecumenical council of a truly global Catholic Church, the influential prelates, intellectual heavyweights, and institutional power and wealth were still disproportionately from continental Europe and the Anglosphere. It was a Council shaped by Louvain theologians, French religious, and Italian bishops, notwithstanding the increasingly confident and active voices of theologians and episcopacies from around the world.

If a Vatican III were to convene in, say, the late 21st century, the intellectual and ecclesial centres in the northern hemisphere would probably still be very important—many Catholic intellectuals from the global South undergo at least part of their academic training in European or North American universities or seminaries. However, the demographic weight of the Catholic world—and increasingly of the episcopacy and the College of

> The Catholic episcopate came together [at Vatican II] to listen and to discern the path for the Church indicated by the Holy Spirit. To doubt the Council is to doubt the intentions of those very Fathers who exercised their collegial power in a solemn manner *cum Petro et sub Petro* ['with Peter and under Peter'] in an ecumenical council, and, in the final analysis, to doubt the Holy Spirit himself who guides the Church.
>
> **Pope Francis**, cover letter accompanying *motu proprio Traditionis Custodes*, 16 July 2021

Cardinals that de facto more and more represent it—would decidedly belong to the global South. The key theologians and important prelates at this hypothetical Vatican III would just as likely come from places like India, Vietnam, and the Philippines as from Spain, the United States, or Poland. Certainly, women would need to have a greatly expanded place as genuine theological contributors and participants, and not merely as silent 'hearers' (i.e. auditors) like they were at Vatican II. A Vatican III would, presumably, find dialogue with Islam in Africa and Pentecostalism in Latin America much more pressing matters than exchanges with Jews or mainline Protestants in Europe and the USA. Mirroring these realities, the reception of Vatican II is shifting out of primarily European-Anglosphere categories and into projects marking the global legacy of the Council—and the paths opened up by such contextualized reception, with all the attendant questions attached. Pope Francis, whatever else his complex legacy will be, has endorsed synodality at every ecclesial level. This ecclesiological path of deliberation and 'listening' will not in itself cause a Vatican III, but it will probably largely condition the procedures the next ecumenical council will adopt and the questions it will take up.

Appendix: the Council's 16 documents

Ad Gentes (7 Dec. 1965)—Decree on the Mission Activity of the Church

Apostolicam Actuositatem (18 Nov. 1965)—Decree on the Apostolate of the Laity

Christus Dominus (28 Oct. 1965)—Decree Concerning the Pastoral Office of Bishops in the Church

Dei Verbum (18 Nov. 1965)—Dogmatic Constitution on Divine Revelation

Dignitatis Humanae (7 Dec. 1965)—Declaration on Religious Freedom

Gaudium et Spes (7 Dec. 1965)—Pastoral Constitution on the Church in the Modern World

Gravissimum Educationis (28 Oct. 1965)—Declaration on Christian Education

Inter Mirifica (4 Dec. 1963)—Decree on the Media of Social Communications

Lumen Gentium (21 Nov. 1964)—Dogmatic Constitution on the Church

Nostra Aetate (28 Oct. 1965)—Declaration on the Relation of the Church to non-Christian Religions

Optatam Totius (28 Oct. 1965)—Decree on Priestly Training

Orientalium Ecclesiarum (21 Nov. 1964)—Decree on the Catholic Churches of the Eastern Rite

Perfectae Caritatis (28 Oct. 1965)—Decree on the Adaptation and Renewal of Religious Life

Presbyterorum Ordinis (7 Dec. 1965)—Decree on the Ministry and Life of Priests

Sacrosanctum Concilium (4 Dec. 1963)—Dogmatic Constitution on the Sacred Liturgy

Unitatis Redintegratio (21 Nov. 1964)—Decree on Ecumenism

Glossary

aggiornamento an Italian word which could be woodenly translated into English as 'updating'. *Aggiornamento* came to be associated with Pope John XXIII and his calls to let 'fresh air' into the Catholic Church through a reinvigoration and representation of the Church's message.

auditor literally, a 'hearer', these were officially recognized guests at the Council. Notably, Vatican II included women and non-Catholic Christians among the auditors.

Aula the 'court' or 'hall'. This is the term used for where the debates in St Peter's Basilica took place.

Curia literally 'household', the Roman Curia refers to the pope's administrative, governing, and at times teaching apparatus in the Holy See.

Magisterium a technical term for the official teaching and governing structures of the Catholic Church. *Magister* is Latin for 'teacher', but the term *Magisterium* only rose to prominence in the 19th century. On the eve of the Council, the term was seen to apply mostly to the papacy and certain organs of the Roman Curia, though it was always recognized that local bishops also participated in the Church's Magisterium.

peritus literally 'expert' in Latin, the *periti* (plural form) were theological experts, usually scholarly priests, who were officially appointed to assist the bishops at Vatican II.

promulgate a technical term for the formal ratification of a council document. Once the final vote on a document was taken, the pope's assent and signature of that final version resulted in 'promulgation'—the final stage of approval which put the document into effect, to eventually be published and disseminated.

ressourcement a French neologism popularized in the decades preceding the Council. *Ressourcement* describes an aspect of reform that involves a searching of historical texts and data (the Bible, the Church Fathers, liturgical heritage, etc.) in order to reapply the theological wisdom of the past to the present.

schema the technical term for a draft document put to a committee or the whole of the Council Fathers for deliberation and eventually voting.

References and further reading

All main documents of Vatican II itself are freely available online at the Vatican's website (<www.vatican.va>), and it is these 'official translations' that we have tended to quote (albeit occasionally flagging our own preferred translation of this term or other). The same is true of most other magisterial texts quoted or cited herein, especially those from the last century or so.

In addition to the texts themselves, there are a number of other pre-eminent sources for analysing and interpreting the Council. These include the official *Acta*, published in 25 bulky volumes as *Acta Synodalia Concilii Vaticani Secundi* (Vatican City: Typis Polyglottis Vaticanus, 1970–96). Of rather more direct utility for the general student is the exhaustive, five-volume *History of Vatican II* (Mayknoll, NY: Orbis, 1995–2006), edited by Giuseppe Alberigo and Joseph Komonchak. Also essential is the five-volume *Commentary on the Documents of Vatican II* (New York: Herder and Herder, 1967–9), edited by Herbert Vorgrimler. This was published soon after the Council, and authored by a host of influential *periti*.

More generally, the Council has been very well served by introductory texts and wide-ranging explorations. Among those we have learned much from ourselves, we include:

Alberigo, Giuseppe. 2006. *A Brief History of Vatican II*, trans. Matthew Sherry (Maryknoll, NY: Orbis Books)

Cummings, Kathleen Sprows, Timothy Matovina, and Robert A. Orsi (eds). 2018. *Catholics in the Vatican II Era: Local Histories of a Global Event* (New York: Cambridge University Press)

Gaillardetz, Richard (ed.). 2020. *The Cambridge Companion to Vatican II* (Cambridge: Cambridge University Press)
Hahnenberg, Edward P. 2007. *A Concise Guide to the Documents of Vatican II* (Ann Arbor, Mich.: Servant Books)
Lamb, Matthew and Matthew Levering (eds). 2008. *Vatican II: Renewal within Tradition* (Oxford: Oxford University Press)

Chapter 1: What is an 'ecumenical council'?

Bellitto, Christopher. 2015. *The General Councils: A History of the Twenty-One Church Councils from Nicaea to Vatican II* (Mahwah, NJ: Paulist Press)
Butler, Christopher. 1967. *The Theology of Vatican II: The Sarum Lectures 1966* (London: Darton, Longman & Todd)
Congar, Yves. 1963. *Report from Rome: On the First Session of the Vatican Council*, trans. A. Manson (London: Geoffrey Chapman)
Harris, Alana and Isobel Ryan. 2020. *Sink or Swim: Catholicism in Sixties Britain through John Ryan's Cartoons* (Durham: Sacristy Press)
König, Franz. 2005. *Open to God, Open to the World*, ed. Christa Pongratz-Lippitt (London: Burns and Oates)
Laffin, Josephine. 2014. 'An Australian Bishop at Vatican II: Matthew Beovich's Council Diary', *Australasian Catholic Record* 91/4, 387–495
MacMullen, Ramsay. 2006. *Voting About God in Early Church Councils* (New Haven: Yale University Press)
O'Malley, John W. 2006. 'Vatican II: Did Anything Happen?', *Theological Studies* 67, 3–33
O'Malley, John W. 2018. *Vatican I: The Council and the Making of the Ultramontane Church* (Cambridge, Mass.: The Belknap Press of Harvard University Press)
Rahner, Karl. [1954] 1967. 'The Christian among Unbelieving Relations', in *Theological Investigations*, vol. 3, trans. Karl-H. and Boniface Kruger (London: Darton, Longman & Todd), 355–72
Tanner, Norman P. 2001. *The Church Councils: A Short History* (New York: Crossroad)
Üffing, Martin. 2013. 'Catholic Mission in Europe 1910–2010', in Stephen B. Bevans (ed.), *A Century of Catholic Mission: Roman Catholic Missiology 1910 to the Present* (Oxford: Regnum), 34–43

Chapter 2: Before the Council: roots of reform

Blanchard, Shaun. 2020. *The Synod of Pistoia and Vatican II: Jansenism and the Struggle for Catholic Reform* (Oxford: Oxford University Press)

Congar, Yves. [1968 edn] 2011. *True and False Reform in the Church*, trans. Paul Philibert. (Collegeville, Minn.: Liturgical Press)

Flynn, Gabriel and Paul D. Murray (eds). 2012. *Ressourcement: A Movement for Renewal in Twentieth-Century Catholic Theology* (Oxford: Oxford University Press)

Krieg, Robert. 1997. *Romano Guardini: A Precursor of Vatican II* (Notre Dame, Ind.: University of Notre Dame Press)

Lehner, Ulrich. 2016. *The Catholic Enlightenment: The Forgotten History of a Global Movement* (Oxford: Oxford University Press)

Mettepeningen, Jürgen. 2010. *Nouvelle Théologie—New Theology: Inheritor of Modernism, Precursor of Vatican II* (London: T&T Clark)

O'Malley, John W. 2012. '"The Hermeneutic of Reform": A Historical Analysis', *Theological Studies* 73, 517–46

Sullivan, Maureen. 2007. *The Road to Vatican II: Key Changes in Theology* (New York: Paulist Press)

Wolf, Hubert. 1998. *Antimodernismus und Modernismus in der Katholischen Kirche: Beiträge zum Theologiegeschichtlichen Vorfeld des II. Vatikanums* (Paderborn: F. Schöningh)

Chapter 3: The event of the Council: what happened and when?

Alberigo, Giuseppe and Joseph Komonchak (eds). 1995–2006. *History of Vatican II*, 5 vols (Maryknoll, NY: Orbis)

Congar, Yves. 2012. *My Journal of the Council*, trans. Mary John Ronayne OP and Mary Cecily Boulding OP (Collegeville, Minn.: Liturgical Press)

Gaillardetz, Richard (ed.). 2020. *The Cambridge Companion to Vatican II* (Cambridge: Cambridge University Press)

Hünermann, Peter and Bernd Jochen Hilberath (eds). 2004–6. *Herders theologischer Kommentar zum Zweiten Vatikanischen Konzil*, 5 vols (Freiburg: Herder)

Küng, Hans. 1963. 'Ecumenical Orientations', *Worship* 37/1, 83–94

Lamb, Matthew and Matthew Levering (eds). 2008. *Vatican II: Renewal within Tradition* (Oxford: Oxford University Press)

McCloskey, Elizabeth. 2007. 'More Than a Footnote: The Footprints of Mary Luke Tobin at Vatican II', *Merton Seasonal* 32/2, 10–33
McEnroy, Carmel E. 2011. *Guests in Their Own House: The Women of Vatican II* (Eugene, Ore.: Wipf and Stock)
O'Malley, John. 2008. *What Happened at Vatican II* (Cambridge, Mass.: The Belknap Press of Harvard University Press)
Ratzinger, Joseph. 1966. *Theological Highlights of Vatican II* (Mahwah, NJ: Paulist Press)
Tobin, Mary Luke. 1985. 'Women in the Church: Vatican II and After', *Ecumenical Review* 37/3, 295–305
Vorgrimler, Herbert (ed.). 1967–9. *Commentary on the Documents of Vatican II*, 5 vols (New York: Herder and Herder)
Wicks, Jared. 2018. *Investigating Vatican II: Its Theologians, Ecumenical Turn, and Biblical Commitment* (Washington, DC: Catholic University of America Press)

Chapter 4: Liturgy

Bouyer, Louis. 1964. *The Liturgy Revived: A Doctrinal Commentary of the Conciliar Constitution on the Liturgy* (South Bend, Ind.: University of Notre Dame Press)
Bullivant, Stephen. 2017. '"Especially in mission territories": New Evangelization and Liturgical (Reform of the) Reform', in Uwe Michael Lang (ed.), *Authentic Liturgical Renewal in Contemporary Perspective* (London: Bloomsbury T&T Clark), 97–107
Bullivant, Stephen. 2019. *Mass Exodus: Catholic Disaffiliation in Britain and America since Vatican II* (Oxford: Oxford University Press)
Cordeiro, Joseph. 1986. 'The Liturgy Constitution *Sacrosanctum Concilium*', in Alberic Stacpoole (ed.), *Vatican II: By Those Who Were There* (London: Geoffrey Chapman, 1986), 187–94
Davies, Michael. 2009 [1980]. *Pope Paul's New Mass* (Kansas City, Mo.: Angelus Press)
Driscoll, Jeremy. 2017. '*Sacrosanctum Concilium* (The Sacred Liturgy)', in Matthew L. Lamb and Matthew Levering (eds), *The Reception of Vatican II* (New York: Oxford University Press), 23–47
Faggioli, Massimo. 2012. *True Reform: Liturgy and Ecclesiology in* Sacrosanctum Concilium (Collegeville, Minn.: Liturgical Press)
Forst, Marion F. [2000] 2013. *Daily Journal of Vatican II* (Dodge City, Kan.: Catholic Diocese of Dodge City)

Garrigou-Lagrange, Réginald. [1938] 1989. *The Three Ages of the Interior Life: Prelude of Eternal Life*, 2 vols (Rockford, Ill.: TAN Books, 1989)

Gribble, Richard. 2009. 'Vatican II and the Church in Uganda: The Contribution of Bishop Vincent J. McCauley, C.S.C.', *Catholic Historical Review* 95/4, 718–40

Gy, Pierre-Marie. 2003. *The Reception of Vatican II Liturgical Reforms in the Life of the Church: The Père Marquette Lecture for 2003* (Milwaukee, Wis.: Marquette University Press)

Jenny, Henri. 1963. 'The Paschal Mystery is Central', *Worship* 37/8, 497–51

Laffin, Josephine. 2014. 'An Australian Bishop at Vatican II: Matthew Beovich's Council Diary', *Australasian Catholic Record* 91/4, 387–495

Lefebvre, Marcel. 2007. *A Bishop Speaks: Writings and Addresses 1963–76* (St Marys, Kan.: Angelus Press)

Magesa, Laurenti. 2018. *The Post-Conciliar Church in Africa: No Turning Back the Clock* (Eugene, Ore.: Pickwick)

Orobator, Agbonkhianmeghe E. 2013. '"After All, Africa is Largely a Nonliterate Continent": The Reception of Vatican II in Africa', *Theological Studies* 74/2, 284–301

Phan, Peter C. 2011. '"Reception" or "Subversion" of Vatican II by the Asian Churches? A New Way of Being Church in Asia', in William Madges (ed.), *Vatican II: Forty Years Later* (Eugene, Ore.: Wipf and Stock), 26–54

Reid, Alcuin. 2005. *The Organic Development of the Liturgy: The Principles of Liturgical Reform and Their Relation to the Twentieth-Century Liturgical Movement Prior to the Second Vatican Council* (San Francisco: Ignatius Press)

Reid, Alcuin. 2017. 'On the Council Floor: The Council Fathers' Debate of the Schema on the Sacred Liturgy', in Uwe Michael Lang (ed.), *Authentic Liturgical Renewal in Contemporary Perspective* (London: Bloomsbury T&T Clark), 125–44

Reid, Alcuin (ed.). 2011. *A Bitter Trial: Evelyn Waugh and John Cardinal Heenan on the Liturgical Changes*, rev. edn (San Francisco: Ignatius Press)

Saigh, Maximos IV. 1963. 'Language in the Liturgy', *Worship* 37/8, 535–8

Schuler, Richard J. 1987. 'Participation', *Sacred Music* 114/4, 7–10

Vaidyanathan, Brandon. 2018. 'The Politics of the Liturgy in the Archdiocese of Bangalore', in Kathleen Sprows Cummings,

Timothy Matovina, and Robert A. Orsi (eds), *Catholics in the Vatican II Era: Local Histories of a Global Event* (New York: Cambridge University Press), 180–205

van Bekkum, Wilhelm. 1963. 'The Liturgical Problems of the Missions', *Worship* 37/8, 501–8

Chapter 5: *Dei Verbum* and divine revelation

Blanchard, Shaun. 2020. *The Synod of Pistoia and Vatican II: Jansenism and the Struggle for Catholic Reform* (Oxford: Oxford University Press)

Gaillardetz, Richard. 2020. 'Revelation', in Richard Gaillardetz (ed.), *The Cambridge Companion to Vatican II* (Cambridge: Cambridge University Press), 155–74

Levering, Matthew. 2017. *An Introduction to Vatican II as an Ongoing Theological Event* (Washington, DC: Catholic University of America Press)

Martin, Francis. 2008. 'Revelation and Its Transmission', in Matthew Lamb and Matthew Levering (eds), *Vatican II: Renewal Within Tradition* (Oxford: Oxford University Press), 55–75

Meszaros, Andrew. 2011. '"*Haec Traditio proficit*": Congar's Reception of Newman in *Dei verbum*, Section 8', *New Blackfriars* 92, 247–54

Norwood, Donald W. 2015. *Reforming Rome: Karl Barth and Vatican II* (Grand Rapids, Mich.: Eerdmans)

O'Collins, Gerald. 2018. *Tradition: Understanding Christian Tradition* (Oxford: Oxford University Press)

Ratzinger, Joseph. 1966. *Theological Highlights of Vatican II* (Mahwah, NJ: Paulist Press)

Ratzinger, Joseph. 1967. 'Dogmatic Constitution on Divine Revelation', in Herbert Vorgrimler et al. (eds), *Commentary on the Documents of Vatican II*, vol. 3 (New York: Herder and Herder), 155–272

Ruggieri, Giuseppe. 1997. 'The First Doctrinal Clash', in Giuseppe Alberigo and Joseph Komonchak (eds), *History of Vatican II*, vol. 2: *The Formation of the Council's Identity: First Period and Intersession, October 1962—September 1963* (Maryknoll, NY: Orbis), 233–66

Somerville Knapman, Hugh (ed.). 2020. *A Limerickal Commentary on the Second Vatican Council* (Waterloo: Arouca Press)

Theobald, Christophe. 2006. 'The Church Under the Word of God', trans. Matthew J. O'Connell, in Giuseppe Alberigo and Joseph A. Komonchak (eds), *History of Vatican II*, vol. 5: *The*

Council and the Transition: The Fourth Period and the End of the Council. September 1965—December 1965 (Maryknoll, NY: Orbis Books), 275–361
Wicks, Jared. 2013. 'Scripture Reading Urged *Vehementer* (DV No. 25): Background and Development', *Theological Studies* 74, 555–80

Chapter 6: Ecclesiology: the nature of the Church

Arinze, Francis. 2013. *The Layperson's Distinctive Role* (San Francisco: Ignatius Press)
Bausenhart, Guido. 2005. 'Christus Dominus: kommentiert von Guido Bausenhart', in Peter Hünermann and Bernd Jochen Hilberath (eds), *Herders theologischer Kommentar zum Zweiten Vatikanischen Konzil*, vol. 3 (Freiburg: Herder), 225–314
Becker, Werner and Johannes Feiner. 1967. 'Decree on Ecumenism', in Herbert Vorgrimler (ed.), *Commentary on the Documents of Vatican II*, vol. 2 (London: Burns and Oates), 1–164
Blanchard, Shaun. 2020. *The Synod of Pistoia and Vatican II: Jansenism and the Struggle for Catholic Reform* (Oxford: Oxford University Press)
Hittinger, Russell. 2008. 'The Declaration on Religious Liberty, *Dignitatis Humanae*', in Matthew Lamb and Matthew Levering (eds), *Vatican II: Renewal Within Tradition* (Oxford: Oxford University Press), 359–82
Lakeland, Paul. 2003. *The Liberation of the Laity: In Search of an Accountable Church* (New York: Continuum)
Miccoli, Giovanni. 2003. 'Two Sensitive Issues: Religious Freedom and the Jews', in Giuseppe Alberigo and Joseph Komonchak (eds), *History of Vatican II*, vol. 4: *The Church as Communion: Third Period and Intersession, September 1964—September 1965* (Maryknoll, NY: Orbis), 95–193
Pavan, Pietro. 1967. 'Declaration on Religious Freedom', in Herbert Vorgrimler (ed.), *Commentary on the Documents of Vatican II*, vol. 4 (London: Burns and Oates), 49–86
Pelotte, Donald E. 1976. *John Courtney Murray: Theologian in Conflict* (New York: Paulist Press)
Phillips, Gerard, Aloys Grillmeier, Karl Rahner, Herbert Vorgrimler, Ferdinand Klostermann, Friedrich Wulf, Otto Semmelroth, and Joseph Ratzinger. 1967. 'Dogmatic Constitution on the Church', in Herbert Vorgrimler (ed.), *Commentary on the Documents of Vatican II*, vol. 1 (London: Burns and Oates), 105–306

Ratzinger, Joseph. 1966. *Theological Highlights of Vatican II* (Mahwah, NJ: Paulist Press)

Rico, Herminio. 2002. *John Paul II and the Legacy of* Dignitatis Humanae (Washington, DC: Georgetown University Press)

Rowland, Tracey. 2020. 'Ecclesiology at the Beginning of the Third Millennium', in Kevin Wagner, M. Isabell Naumann, and Peter John McGregor (eds), *Ecclesiology at the Beginning of the Third Millennium* (Eugene, Ore.: Pickwick Publications), 1–28

Schindler, David and Nicholas Healy. 2015. *Freedom, Truth, and Human Dignity: The Second Vatican Council's Declaration on Religious Freedom. A New Translation, Redaction History, and Interpretation of* Dignitatis Humanae (Grand Rapids, Mich.: Eerdmans)

Stayne, John. 2020. 'The Contribution of Francis A. Sullivan, SJ to a Deeper Understanding of Charisms in the Church', *Theological Studies* 81, 810–27

Sullivan, Francis A. 1975. 'The Ecclesiological Context of the Charismatic Renewal', in Kilian McDonnell (ed.), *The Holy Spirit and Power: The Catholic Charismatic Renewal* (Garden City, NY: Doubleday and Co.), 119–38

Sullivan, Francis A. 2002. 'The Teaching Authority of Episcopal Conferences', *Theological Studies* 63, 472–93

Sullivan, Francis A. 2006. 'A Response to Karl Becker, S.J., on the Meaning of *Subsistit In*', *Theological Studies* 67, 395–409

Tagle, Luis Antonio. 1993. 'Episcopal Collegiality and the Ecclesiological Project of Vatican II', *Landas* 7, 149–60

Tagle, Luis Antonio. 2003. 'The "Black Week" of Vatican II (14–21 November 1964)', in Giuseppe Alberigo and Joseph Komonchak (eds), *History of Vatican II*, vol. 4: *The Church as Communion: Third Period and Intersession, September 1964—September 1965* (Maryknoll, NY: Orbis), 388–452

Tanner, Norman. 2000. 'The Church in the World (Ecclesia Ad Extra)', in Giuseppe Alberigo and Joseph Komonchak (eds), *History of Vatican II*, vol. 3: *The Mature Council: Second Session and Intersession, September 1963—September 1964* (Maryknoll, NY: Orbis), 275–388

Wicks, Jared. 2012. 'Vatican II's Turn in 1963: Toward Renewing Catholic Ecclesiology and Validating Catholic Ecumenical Engagement', *Josephinum Journal of Theology* 19/2, 1–13

Wood, Susan K. 2020. 'Ecumenism', in Richard Gaillardetz (ed.), *The Cambridge Companion to Vatican II* (Cambridge: Cambridge University Press), 282–302

Chapter 7: Church and world

Anderson, Floyd (ed.). 1965. *Council Daybook: Vatican II, Sessions 1 and 2* (Washington, DC: National Catholic Welfare Conference)

Anderson, Floyd (ed.). 1965. *Council Daybook: Vatican II, Session 3* (Washington, DC: National Catholic Welfare Conference)

Baum, Gregory. 2015. 'The Fiftieth Anniversary of *Nostra Aetate*', *Journal of Ecumenical Studies* 50/4, 525–8

Beck, Ashley. 2014. *Benedict XV & World War I* (London: Catholic Truth Society)

Congar, Yves. 1963. *Report from Rome: On the First Session of the Vatican Council* (London: Geoffrey Chapman)

Day, Dorothy. 1965. 'On Pilgrimage', *The Catholic Worker*, December

D'Costa, Gavin. 2014. *Vatican II: Catholic Doctrines on Jews and Muslims* (Oxford: Oxford University Press)

de Lubac, Henri. 2015. *Vatican Council Notebooks I*, trans. Andrew Stefanelli and Anne Englund Nash (San Francisco: Ignatius Press)

de Lubac, Henri. 2016. *Vatican Council Notebooks*, vol. 2, trans. Anne Englund Nash (San Francisco: Ignatius Press)

Flessati, Valerie. 1991. 'PAX: The History of a Catholic Peace Society in Britain, 1936–1971', PhD thesis, University of Bradford

Hadas, Edward. 2020. *Counsels of Imperfection: Thinking Through Catholic Social Teaching* (Washington, DC: Catholic University of America Press)

Hinsdale, Mary Ann. 2016. 'Vatican II and Feminism: Recovered Memories and Refreshed Hopes', *Toronto Journal of Theology* 32/2, 251–72

Hünermann, Peter. 2006. 'The Final Weeks of the Council', trans. Matthew J. O'Connell, in Giuseppe Alberigo and Joseph A. Komonchak (eds), *History of Vatican II*, vol. 5: *The Council and the Transition. The Fourth Period and the End of the Council. September 1965–December 1965* (Maryknoll, NY: Orbis Books), 363–483

Jarvis, Edward. 2018. *Sede Vacante: The Life and Legacy of Archbishop Thục* (San Francisco: Apocryphile Press)

Lefebvre, Marcel. 2007. *A Bishop Speaks: Writings and Addresses 1963–76* (St Marys, Kan.: Angelus Press)

McEnroy, Carmel E. 2011. *Guests in Their Own House: The Women of Vatican II* (Eugene, Ore.: Wipf and Stock)

Melloni, Alberto. 2007. '*Nostra Aetate* and the Discovery of the Sacrament of Otherness', in Philip A. Cunningham,

Norbert J. Hoffman, and Joseph A. Sievers (eds), *The Catholic Church and the Jewish People: Recent Reflections from Rome* (New York: Fordham University Press), 129–51

Oesterreicher, John M. 1971. *The Rediscovery of Judaism: A Re-Examination of the Conciliar Statement on the Jews* (South Orange, NJ: Institute of Judaeo-Christian Studies)

Ottaviani, Alfredo. 1949. 'The Future of Offensive War', *Blackfriars* 30/354, 415–50

Ratzinger, Joseph. 1966. *Theological Highlights of Vatican II* (Mahwah, NJ: Paulist Press)

Routhier, Gilles. 2006. 'Finishing the Work Begun: The Trying Experience of the Fourth Period', trans. Matthew J. O'Connell, in Giuseppe Alberigo and Joseph A. Komonchak (eds), *History of Vatican II*, vol. 5: *The Council and the Transition. The Fourth Period and the End of the Council. September 1965–December 1965* (Maryknoll, NY: Orbis Books), 49–184

Somerville Knapman, Hugh (ed.). 2020. *A Limerickal Commentary on the Second Vatican Council* (Waterloo: Arouca Press)

Tanner, Norman. 2005. *The Church and the World:* Gaudium et Spes, Inter Mirifica (Mahwah, NJ: Paulist Press)

Thornton, Brian. 2014. 'Voice for Truth: Archbishop Denis Hurley and the Second Vatican Council', unpublished Master thesis, St Michael's College, Toronto

Tobias, Norman C. 2019. *Jewish Conscience of the Church: Jules Isaac and the Second Vatican Council* (London: Palgrave Macmillan)

Wilde, Melissa J. 2007. *Vatican II: A Sociological Analysis of Religious Change* (Princeton: Princeton University Press)

Chapter 8: Conciliar 'hermeneutics': making sense of the debates over Vatican II

Alberigo, Giuseppe, Jean-Pierre Jossua, and Joseph A. Komonchak. 1987. *The Reception of Vatican II*, trans. Matthew J. O'Connell (Washington, DC: Catholic University of America Press)

Blanchard, Shaun. 2021. 'Traditionis Custodes Was Never Merely About the Liturgy', *Church Life Journal* (online publication of the McGrath Institute for Church Life, University of Notre Dame) 2 August 2021

Blanchard, Shaun. 2020. *The Synod of Pistoia and Vatican II: Jansenism and the Struggle for Catholic Reform* (Oxford: Oxford University Press)

Bouyer, Louis. 1969. *The Decomposition of Catholicism*, trans. Charles Underhill (London: Sands & Co.)
Bullivant, Stephen. 2019. *Mass Exodus: Catholic Disaffiliation in Britain and America since Vatican II* (Oxford: Oxford University Press)
Comblin, José. 2004. *People of God*, ed. and trans. Phillip Berryman (Maryknoll, NY: Orbis Books)
D'Costa, Gavin. 2014. *Vatican II: Catholic Doctrines on Jews and Muslims* (Oxford: Oxford University Press)
Dulles, Avery. 1988. *The Reshaping of Catholicism: Current Challenges in the Theology of Church* (San Francisco: Harper & Row)
Faggioli, Massimo. 2012. *Vatican II: The Battle for Meaning* (New York: Paulist Press)
Faggioli, Massimo. 2015. *A Council for the Global Church: Receiving Vatican II in History* (Minneapolis, Minn.: Fortress Press)
Guarino, Thomas. 2018. *The Disputed Teachings of Vatican II: Continuity and Reversal in Catholic Doctrine* (Grand Rapids, Mich.: Eerdmans)
Greeley, Andrew. 2004. *The Catholic Revolution: New Wine, Old Wineskins, and the Second Vatican Council* (Berkeley: University of California Press)
Hinsdale, Mary Ann. 2016. 'Vatican II and Feminism: Recovered Memories and Refreshed Hopes', *Toronto Journal of Theology* 32/2, 251–72
Hünermann, Peter (ed.). 2009. *Exkommunikation oder Kommunikation? Der Weg der Kirche nach dem. II Vatikanum und die Pius-Brüder* (Freiburg i.B.: Herder)
O'Malley, John W. 2012. '"The Hermeneutic of Reform": A Historical Analysis', *Theological Studies* 73, 517–46
Ratzinger, Joseph. 1987. *Principles of Catholic Theology* (San Francisco: Ignatius Press)
Rhonheimer, Martin. 2011. 'Benedict XVI's "Hermeneutic of Reform" and Religious Freedom', *Nova et Vetera* 9/4, 1029–54
Rush, Ormond. 2004. *Still Interpreting Vatican II: Some Hermeneutical Principles* (Mahwah, NJ: Paulist Press)
Rush, Ormond. 2019. *The Vision of Vatican II: Its Fundamental Principles* (Collegeville, Minn.: Liturgical Press)
Schultenover, David (ed.). 2007. *Vatican II: Did Anything Happen?* (New York: Continuum)
Steinfels, Peter. 2003. *A People Adrift: The Crisis of the Roman Catholic Church in America* (New York: Simon & Schuster)

Index

For the benefit of digital users, indexed terms that span two pages (e.g., 52–53) may, on occasion, appear on only one of those pages.

A

B

C

D

E

S

T

U

V

W

CATHOLICISM

A Very Short Introduction

Gerald O'Collins

Despite a long history of external threats and internal strife, the Roman Catholic Church and the broader reality of Catholicism remain a vast and valuable presence into the third millennium of world history. What are the origins of the Catholic Church? How has Catholicism changed and adapted to such vast and diverse cultural influences over the centuries? What great challenges does the Catholic Church now face in the twenty-first century, both within its own life and in its relation to others around the world? In this Very Short Introduction, Gerald O'Collins draws on the best current scholarship available to answer these questions and to present, in clear and accessible language, a fresh introduction to the largest and oldest institution in the world.

www.oup.com/vsi

Christian Ethics

A Very Short Introduction

D. Stephen Long

This *Very Short Introduction* to Christian ethics introduces the topic by examining its sources and historical basis. D. Stephen Long presents a discussion of the relationship between Christian ethics, modern, and postmodern ethics, and explores practical issues including sex, money, and power. Long recognises the inherent difficulties in bringing together 'Christian' and 'ethics' but argues that this is an important task for both the Christian faith and for ethics. Arguing that Christian ethics are not a precise science, but the cultivation of practical wisdom from a range of sources, Long also discusses some of the failures of the Christian tradition, including the crusades, the conquest, slavery, inquisitions, and the Galileo affair.

www.oup.com/vsi

THE NEW TESTAMENT

A Very Short Introduction

Luke Timothy Johnson

As part of the Christian Bible, the New Testament is at once widely influential and increasingly unknown. Those who want to know the basics can find in this introduction the sort of information that locates these ancient writings in their historical and literary context. In addition to providing the broad conceptual and factual framework for the New Testament — including the process by which distinct compositions became a sacred book — this introduction provides as well a more detailed examination of specific compositions that have had particularly strong influence, including Paul's letters to the Corinthians and Romans, the four Gospels, and the Book of Revelation.

www.oup.com/vsi

THE NEW TESTAMENT AS LITERATURE

A Very Short Introduction

Kyle Keefer

Looking at the New Testament through the lens of literary study, Kyle Keefer offers an engrossing exploration of this revered religious text as a work of literature, but also keeps in focus its theological ramifications. Unique among books that examine the Bible as literature, this brilliantly compact introduction offers an intriguing double-edged look at this universal text--a religiously informed literary analysis. The book first explores the major sections of the New Testament--the gospels, Paul's letters, and Revelation--as individual literary documents. Keefer shows how, in such familiar stories as the parable of the Good Samaritan, a literary analysis can uncover an unexpected complexity to what seems a simple, straightforward tale.

BIBLICAL ARCHAEOLOGY

A Very Short Introduction

Eric H. Cline

Archaeologist Eric H. Cline here offers a complete overview of this exciting field. He discusses the early pioneers, the origins of biblical archaeology as a discipline, and the major controversies that first prompted explorers to go in search of sites that would "prove" the Bible. He then surveys some of the most well-known modern archaeologists, the sites that are essential sources of knowledge for biblical archaeology, and some of the most important discoveries that have been made in the last half century, including the Dead Sea Scrolls and the Tel Dan Stele.

www.oup.com/vsi

PENTECOSTALISM
A Very Short Introduction
William K. Kay

In religious terms Pentecostalism was probably the most vibrant and rapidly-growing religious movement of the 20th century. Starting as a revivalistic and renewal movement within Christianity, it encircled the globe in less than 25 years and grew in North America and then in those parts of the world with the highest birth-rates. Characterised by speaking in tongues, miracles, television evangelism and megachurches, it is also noted for its small-group meetings, empowerment of individuals, liberation of women and humanitarian concerns. William K Kay outlines the origins and growth of Pentecostalism, looking at not only the theological aspects of the movement, but also the sociological influences of its political and humanitarian viewpoints.

www.oup.com/vsi

THE APOCRYPHAL GOSPELS

A Very Short Introduction

Paul Foster

This *Very Short Introduction* offers a clear, accessible, and concise account of the apocryphal gospels - exploring their origins, their discovery, and discussing how the various texts have been interpreted both by the Church and beyond. Paul Foster shows how the apocryphal gospels reflect the diversity that existed within early Christianity, and examines the extent to which they can be used to reconstruct an accurate portrait of the historical Jesus. Including discussions of controversies and case-studies such as the alleged hoax surrounding the discovery of Secret Mark, Foster concludes that the non-canonical texts, considered in the correct context, offer us an important window on the vibrant and multi-faceted face of early Christianity.

> 'He writes with elegance and clarity, and presents . . . complex arguments . . . with simplicity and grace.'
>
> **Baptist Times**

www.oup.com/vsi

AGNOSTICISM

A Very Short Introduction

Robin Le Poidevin

What is agnosticism? Is it just the 'don't know' position on God, or is there more to it than this? Is it a belief, or merely the absence of belief? Who were the first to call themselves 'agnostics'? These are just some of the questions that Robin Le Poidevin considers in this *Very Short Introduction*. He sets the philosophical case for agnosticism and explores it as a historical and cultural phenomenon. What emerges is a much more sophisticated, and much more interesting, attitude than a simple failure to either commit to, or reject, religious belief. Le Poidevin challenges some preconceptions and assumptions among both believers and non-atheists, and invites the reader to rethink their own position on the issues.

www.oup.com/vsi

Religion in America

A Very Short Introduction

Timothy Beal

Timothy Beal describes many aspects of religion in contemporary America that are typically ignored in other books on the subject, including religion in popular culture and counter-cultural groups; the growing phenomenon of "hybrid" religious identities, both individual and collective; the expanding numbers of new religious movements, or NRMs, in America; and interesting examples of "outsider religion." He also offers an engaging overview of the history of religion in America, from Native American traditions to the present day. Finally, Beal highlights the three major forces shaping the present and future of religion in America.

www.oup.com/vsi

THOMAS AQUINAS

A Very Short Introduction

Fergus Kerr

Thomas Aquinas, an Italian Catholic priest in the early thirteenth century, is considered to be one of the great Christian thinkers who had, and who still has, a profound influence on Western thought. He was a controversial figure who was exposed and engaged in conflict. This *Very Short Introduction* looks at Aquinas in a historical context, and explores the Church and culture into which Aquinas was born. It considers Aquinas as philosopher, and looks at the relationship between philosophy and religion in the thirteenth century. Fergus Kerr, in this engaging and informative introduction, will make *The Summa Theologiae*, Aquinas's greatest single work, accessible to new readers. It will also reflect on the importance of Thomas Aquinas in modern debates and asks why Aquinas matters now.

SCIENCE AND RELIGION

A Very Short Introduction

Thomas Dixon

The debate between science and religion is never out of the news: emotions run high, fuelled by polemical bestsellers and, at the other end of the spectrum, high-profile campaigns to teach 'Intelligent Design' in schools. Yet there is much more to the debate than the clash of these extremes. As Thomas Dixon shows in this balanced and thought-provoking introduction, many have seen harmony rather than conflict between faith and science. He explores not only the key philosophical questions that underlie the debate, but also the social, political, and ethical contexts that have made 'science and religion' such a fraught and interesting topic in the modern world, offering perspectives from non-Christian religions and examples from across the physical, biological, and social sciences.

> 'A rich introductory text . . . on the study of relations of science and religion.'
>
> **R. P. Whaite, Metascience**

www.oup.com/vsi

PAGANISM

A Very Short Introduction

Owen Davies

This *Very Short Introduction* explores the meaning of paganism - through a chronological overview of the attitudes towards its practices and beliefs - from the ancient world through to the present day. Owen Davies largely looks at paganism through the eyes of the Christian world, and how, over the centuries, notions and representations of its nature were shaped by religious conflict, power struggles, colonialism, and scholarship. Despite the expansion of Christianity and Islam, Pagan cultures continue to exist around the world, whilst in the West new formations of paganism constitute one of the fastest-growing religions.

www.oup.com/vsi

THE REFORMATION
A Very Short Introduction
Peter Marshall

The Reformation transformed Europe, and left an indelible mark on the modern world. It began as an argument about what Christians needed to do to be saved, but rapidly engulfed society in a series of fundamental changes. This *Very Short Introduction* provides a lively and up-to-date guide to the process. Peter Marshall argues that the Reformation was not a solely European phenomenon, but that varieties of faith exported from Europe transformed Christianity into a truly world religion. It explains doctrinal debates in a clear and non-technical way, but is equally concerned to demonstrate the effects the Reformation had on politics, society, art, and minorities.

www.oup.com/vsi